GULF COAST

Tanchipa ▲

Altamira ▲
Panuco ▲   Las Flores ▲
Tamuin ▲
rde ▲   Tempoal ▲

Tepetzintla ▲

El Tajín ▲

Tulancingo ▲

Misantla ▲

Teotihuácan ▲

Cempoala ▲
MEXICO CITY   El Faisán ▲
atilco   Remojadas ▲
Cuicuilco
Gualupita   Cholula
chicalco
Chalcacingo   Tehuacán ▲   Nopiloa
Cerro de las Mesas ▲
Tres Zapotes ▲   Santiago Tuxtla ▲   Comalcalco ▲
Acayucan ▲   La Venta ▲   Jonuta ▲
Quiotepec ▲   Minatitlán ▲
a   San Lorenzo ▲
OAXACA REGION

Teposcocula ▲
Tlaxiaco ▲   Monte Albán ▲   Yagul ▲
Zaachila ▲   Mitla ▲
Ayutla ▲

Piedra ▲   Tutotepec ▲
Labrada

Juchitán ▲

Tonalá ▲

REGION MAYA

Chiapa de Corzo ▲
Chincultic ▲

Izapa ▲
Ocos ▲

GUATEMALA

Dzibilchaltun ▲
Chichen Itzá ▲
Mayapán ▲   Cobá ▲
Uxmal ▲   Tulum ▲
Kabah ▲   Labná ▲
Jaina ▲
Edzná ▲   Dzibilnocac ▲

Xpuhil ▲

Palenque ▲
Piedras Negras ▲
Yaxchilan ▲
Bonampak ▲

Uaxactun ▲
Tikal ▲

BRITISH HONDURAS

Zaculeu ▲

Quirigua ▲
Copán ▲

HONDURAS

Kaminaljuyu ▲
El Baúl ▲
S. Lucía Cozulmahuapa ▲

Luis Covarrubias

THE NATIONAL MUSEUM OF ANTHROPOLOGY

MEXICO

PEDRO RAMIREZ VAZQUEZ

LUIS AVELEYRA, RAMON PIÑA CHAN, DEMETRIO SODI, RICARDO DE ROBINA AND ALFONSO CASO
CAPTIONS BY SALVADOR NOVO

THE NATIONAL MUSEUM OF ANTHROPOLOGY

MEXICO

Art · Architecture · Archaeology · Anthropology

INTRODUCTION BY IGNACIO BERNAL

DESIGNED AND EDITED BY BEATRICE TRUEBLOOD

HARRY N. ABRAMS, INC., NEW YORK
IN ASSOCIATION WITH HELVETICA PRESS, INC.

Translations from the Spanish text: Mary Jean Labadie, Aza Zatz

PRODUCTION SUPERVISED BY EDITA S.A., LAUSANNE

A HELVETICA PRESS PRODUCTION

© by Pedro Ramírez Vázquez, 1968

Library of Congress card number: 68-19150

PRINTED IN SWITZERLAND
BOUND IN THE NETHERLANDS

CONTENTS

PREFACE

The necessity of devoting a special book to Mexico's National Museum of Anthropology became manifest soon after its inauguration. The great number of national and foreign visitors to its halls as well as the countless inquiries for specific information regarding its collections, installations and other services, made evident that the interest aroused by the new institution extended well beyond its own walls.

The National Museum of Anthropology is certainly the museum of Mexico. It fulfills at least three inter-related purposes. Here the visitor finds a unique collection of art works ranging in age from pre-historic times to today, displayed in a lucidly understandable way. The Museum is a living lesson in art and history, and this educational purpose is naturally complemented by a second: the Museum supports scientific and historical research on each of the different cultures treated in its rooms, the results of which are readily available to scholars and the general public alike. Thus, while providing a complete image of the ancient pre-Hispanic civilizations, the Museum maintains an interest and promotes the continuing study not only of the nation's past but of its present, nourished by that past and in a continuous process of transformation from it. In addition to enjoying its displays, no visitor to the Museum fails to become aware of the building itself, a piece of work organically conceived within Chapultepec Park, the most ancient and one of the most magnificent parks in the New World.

This book aspires to reflect the functions of the Museum itself by maintaining its characteristics and by giving a complete picture of it. To realize this intention, the sections of this book follow the order of the Museum's halls, as a visitor would approach them, setting forth in each one one civilization in all of its cultural aspects and time horizon. In this way, the reader will be able to share the same experience as the visitor. The Museum's vast photographic archives have been used for this purpose and the reader will not fail to note that even as ancient Mexico is made visible, so is the living population of contemporary Mexico, without whose steady labor the building would not have been completed in only nineteen months.

No work of this complexity and scope could have been accomplished without the collaboration of many persons. I wish to express my appreciation to all the technical and administrative personnel of the Museum; in particular to Mrs. Margarita Laris, Mrs. Susana Peres, Mrs. Lilia Trejo de Aveleyra, Mr. Carlo Saenz, Mr. Jorge Cabrera and Mr. Juan de los Reyes. Dr. Eusebio Dávalos Hurtado, Director of the National Institute of Anthropology and History, Dr. Ignacio Bernal, Director of the Museum of Anthropology and Dr. Luis Aveleyra devoted a great deal of their time to the revision of the archaeological texts, a task for which I am especially grateful, as well as to Mrs. Lina Odena Güemes, for her revision of the ethnographic concepts, Mrs. Susana Esponda for her general assistance, and Dr. Eugenio Villa Caña whose editing and advice were most valuable. I am also grateful for the collaboration of the following professors of the School of Ethnography of the Museum, upon whose writings and research the ethnographic chapters of this book were based: Barbara Dahlgren Jordan, Guillermo Bonfil Batalla, Margarita Nolasco, Lina O. Güemes de Muñoz and Mercedes Olivera de Vázquez.

PEDRO RAMÍREZ VÁZQUEZ.

INTRODUCTION

The visionary idea of a statesman, President Adolfo López Mateos, and the deft and imaginative direction of an ambitious project made it possible for the National Museum of Anthropology—begun in February, 1963—to open its doors to the public in September, 1964. Like all great endeavors, however, realization of the astonishing concept of this museum was favored by philosophical, psychological, social and political factors that reach much farther back in the national past. In order to understand these, it is necessary to relate, however briefly, the story of how a modest germinal intuition developed into the great idea that is the monument which exists today. We will not properly appreciate the imagination and will of this remarkable statesman unless we imagine them within the context of Mexican history in which the museum has its truest significance. It was he, of course, who pressed the button that started the machinery, and his continued careful guidance caused this machinery to function admirably; still, his personal efforts were supported by a social and historical process that has lasted almost two hundred years—a process that helps to explain not only the origins of the museum but also a substantial part of the country's own history.

Mexico has both the glory and the burden of inheriting two civilizations, the Hispanic and the Indian or Mesoamerican, and its destiny has consisted in comprehending both and fusing them into a single national culture. Soon after the Spanish Conquest, the conquistadors, and later the missionaries, realized the need for gaining some understanding of the vanquished culture. They knew that it represented an inescapable part of their era and of the colony which was later to evolve into the modern nation of Mexico.

This first conscious awareness of the native component and its contribution to civilization corresponds to what we might call the first stage of a growing national identity. The second phase occurred in the second half of the eighteenth century, when a number of enlightened individuals born in Mexican territory became interested in its antiquities, history and ethnography. It is relevant, moreover, that these men called themselves Mexicans. They no longer thought of themselves as inhabitants of "New Spain," but rather as a wholly new group which was Spanish in culture and spirit but which recognized that spirit as already modified by its blending with the Indian spirit and culture. They began to realize that these merging streams would eventually form a new citizen. Not surprisingly it was during this period that the first studies of Mesoamerican archaeological monuments were made, at times sponsored by the Spanish rulers themselves. For the first time, some care was taken with the monoliths found by chance in various locations—for instance in the Zócalo, the main square of Mexico City—for the purpose of studying them and obtaining an understanding of the ancient cultures of the land. This desire to define and appreciate the native contribution became visible in many ways.

Shortly before 1775, Viceroy Bucareli, the colonial governor, ordered the transfer to the University of "the most exquisite relics of Mexican antiquity," including documents in European script and in hieroglyphics, that had been collected many years earlier by Lorenzo Boturini. On August 13, 1790, the noted sculpture of Coatlicue was discovered in the Zócalo or main public square, and was also taken to the University. On December 17 of the same year workers found the Piedra del Sol (the Sun Stone), or "Aztec Calendar." These two monuments furnished the basis for a study of the "two stones" by Antonio de León y Gama. Actually there were six stones involved in his work, since four additional carved stones were found in the Zócalo between December, 1791, and June, 1792. These and other minor objects were to form the nucleus of the future museum, and León y Gama's were the first studies based on ancient finds.

Toward the end of the colonial period, Viceroy Iturrigaray established a Board of Antiquities. Indian antiquities were no longer worthless items to be thrown away, but became valuable relics to be preserved. However relics collected by the end of the eighteenth century were to undergo many critical turns of fortune: disdained by some, considered in appalling taste by others, and admired deeply by a few.

The wars for independence in the nineteenth century and the increasing antipathy towards Spain produced a third stage of growing self-identity, marked by the Mexican's becoming interested once again in his original culture. The next step was the founding of an archaeological museum by the decrees of two

The building at 13 Moneda Street, adjoining the Palace of the Viceroy, was built in 1734. One of the best examples of the architectural style of its period, the building served for many years as the colonial mint. From 1866 to 1964 it housed the Museum of Anthropology.

President Adolfo López Mateos (*third from left*), is accompanied by the Secretary of Public Education, Jaime Torres Bodet (*second from left*), Mayor Ernesto P. Uruchurtu of Mexico City (*extreme left*) and Pedro Ramírez Vázquez (*second from right*), planner and director of the project, at the inauguration of the National Museum of Anthropology in September, 1964.

presidents, Guadalupe Victoria and Anastasio Bustamante, an undertaking furthered by the efforts of the great historian Lucas Alaman—the "founder of the Mexican museum," as he was called by Carlos Maria de Bustamante, a distinguished editor of the period.

The tiny University museum referred to above already housed a magnificent archaeological testimony of Mexico's past. During the first half of the nineteenth century there were several printings and notices of Nebel's collection of illustrations, *Mexico and its Environs*. In one of these notices José Fernando Ramírez described in great detail a very interesting plate that showed, in romantic disarray, the chief objects on display in what was then the National Museum. Icaza and Gondra began to publish these drawings serially in 1827; their publishing program, unfortunately, was not completed. Deficient as it may have been by present-day standards, it would have constituted the first catalogue of the infant museum.

It cannot be said that the museum's true significance and potential were really understood at that period, for it did not in fact then have national importance. We may grant that it sheltered, in the typical disordered manner of the day, a sizable number of objects, which were gradually augmented. But the principal objective of a museum—to present the ancient civilization and its legacy to a new generation in such a way as to make them understood and appreciated as an important part of the national spirit, thereby furnishing a testimonial to the dignity and worth of the Indian peoples and their culture—this purpose had not yet fully emerged. When, in 1865, Emperor Maximilian had the museum moved to its first quarters on Moneda Street, as part of his campaign to elevate the descendants of Mexico's Indian population, his move was primarily political in motivation; his was but an embryo of an idea. After that time, other and opposing ideas arose, among them the rather outlandish one of insisting upon a whole-hearted return to the Indian past. Fortunately, this antihistorical idea was not shared by the Moneda Street institution; silently, it continued to improve throughout the rest of the nineteenth century. It became the repository of scientific knowledge concerning the ancient Indian groups and it thus promoted genuine, though rather incomplete, understanding of Mesoamerican civilization. At any rate, a real step had been taken towards a more thorough understanding of the Indian heritage as an indispensable part of the national culture.

Since the Revolution of 1910 Mexicans have begun to see their double cultural legacy much more clearly, recognizing the importance of both of its components. It is widely acknowledged that modern day Mexico is the result of a fusion of two old and diverse cultures, and that it is this indissoluble mixture which gives Mexico its unique national character. But how could this meaningful fusion, and particularly the qualities of the indigenous culture (for the Hispanic element has long been well known), be understood and given contemporary validity, if its relics were not studied, if archaeological excavations were not organized to discover the material remains that undoubtedly are still scattered throughout Mexico, and if such artefacts were not brought together and properly preserved and exhibited? It was absolutely essential, then, to create a museum such as this. The synthesis achieved in the imaginative and carefully planned display of its collections transcends the more restricted interests of archaeology or history and constitutes a broader endeavor, one of truly national self-identity.

And yet, the splendor of the building, its inherent attraction to Mexican and foreigner alike, the beauty of the objects therein contained, the appropriateness of their setting, the undeniable evidence of official approbation and popular interest—these will not in themselves, no matter how important they may be, bring about the institution's deepest and most significant purposes. Physical enhancement of the works on exhibit, assurance of governmental support, gratifyingly large attendance—these facts must always be accompanied by constant and ever-increasing research programs and publications, for only continual and related study can uncover the true meanings that will yield us a maximum understanding of our ancient civilizations from which we may set forth their positive and negative contributions to the contemporary world. The museum is a house for the past but it is also a window for the future.

IGNACIO BERNAL
DIRECTOR OF THE NATIONAL MUSEUM OF ANTHROPOLOGY

Dedication plaque above the entrance of the new museum.

The Mexican nation erects this monument in honor of the great cultures that flourished during the pre-Columbian era in regions that now form part of the Republic of Mexico.

In the presence of the vestiges of those cultures, contemporary Mexico pays tribute to indigenous Mexico, in whose expression it discerns the characteristics of its national identity.

Mexico City, 17 September, 1964
Adolfo López Mateos
President of Mexico

13

The rain god Tlaloc, from Coatlinchán (State of Mexico): height, ca. 23 feet. Teotihuacán culture, 4th-6th century A.D. Weighing 168 tons, and thus the largest existing monolith in the Americas, this colossal image was never finished by the stone carvers who were possibly making it for Teotihuacán. The statue, probably abandoned in a ravine near the village of Coatlinchán, now stands, a solemn, imposing and majestic guard, at the entrance of the National Museum of Anthropology and has become the popular symbol of that great cultural repository.

I. THE ARCHITECTURE OF THE MUSEUM

The function of architecture is to provide the spaces man requires for living. This goal is ennobled when the purpose becomes that of creating a place for the treasure of his cultural heritage.

PEDRO RAMÍREZ VÁZQUEZ.

The architectural problem presented by the National Museum of Anthropology had two particular and equally important requirements: the special demands of a building functioning as a museum and the dignified housing and display of a cultural legacy within an architectural expression that was to be contemporary yet not alien to that legacy. To achieve these aims, it was necessary to search for and re-evaluate the nearly forgotten tradition of Mexican architecture, reaching back to its pre-Hispanic past: once these constant elements of tradition were established, our purpose became that of preserving and continuing them, even though their formal solution might not be so adopted. We do much the same thing when we respect and adhere to certain unchanging spiritual norms of our grandfathers without necessarily keeping their manner of dress.

In examining these unchanging values, it became evident that pre-Hispanic, colonial and modern architecture in Mexico has certain elements, or underlying concepts in common, in spite of differences in technique and specific formal solutions: for example, influence of the geographical environment, integration into the landscape, generous use of space, preservation of the natural colors and textures of materials, a plastic continuity perpetuated through the handiwork of the artisan and modes of construction that are characterized by an ambition for permanence and boldness of design.

If architecture is accepted as a faithful reflection of the geographical, technological, economic and social conditions of its time and place, it may be assumed that specific environment constants such as landscape, climate and other natural elements would influence the architecture created therein.

The broad, open spaces typical of pre-Hispanic architectural ensembles in Mexico, whether situated in a valley or on a plateau, are one such reflection of the profound respect landscape has inspired in man and of his communion with the natural world. Pre-Hispanic architects in Mesoamerica never created a structure that conflicted with its surroundings.

The Mexican, in whom two profoundly religious traditions are fused, inherited from both a concept of architecture oriented toward eternity. It is hard to conceive of Teotihuacán, Monte Albán, or Uxmal, without imagining in their Indian builders a desire to build works for all time. Thus, the Mexican's love of the landscape, expressed in a striving for harmony between architecture and environment, began as part of an exalted conception of man, which was not limited to his physical and individual dimension alone, but extended to encompass his dignity as a person in the grandeur of his collective expression. Such conception is clearly recognizable in the Avenue of the Dead in Teotihuacán, and at Monte Albán and other architectural sites. Spaces and masses were planned with a careful eye to dignifying the great multitudes that would congregate in these ritual centers. For expressing the hierarchical nature of the sacred cult, ceremonies were oriented on two different planes: along the vertical axis, the structure exalts divinity; through its horizontals, man remains linked to the earth. Thus architecture, open spaces, and landscape are all fused into a single and indivisible whole.

During the rule of the viceroys, the traditional Indian sensibility survived in imaginative plastic creations, notwithstanding the growing European influence. The indigenous concept of much open space in

The influence of the Governor's Palace in Uxmal, built about a thousand years ago by remarkable Mayan architects, is reflected in contemporary style in the massive dignity and ornamentation of the new National Museum of Anthropology.

architecture maintained its importance and inspired such original solutions as the open chapel set in the courtyard of churches. Gradually, however, European influence was assimilated by both Indians and mestizos. But in modern-day Mexican architecture a like respect for landscape and a generous use of open space remain constant features of tradition. The University City of the nation's capital, in particular,

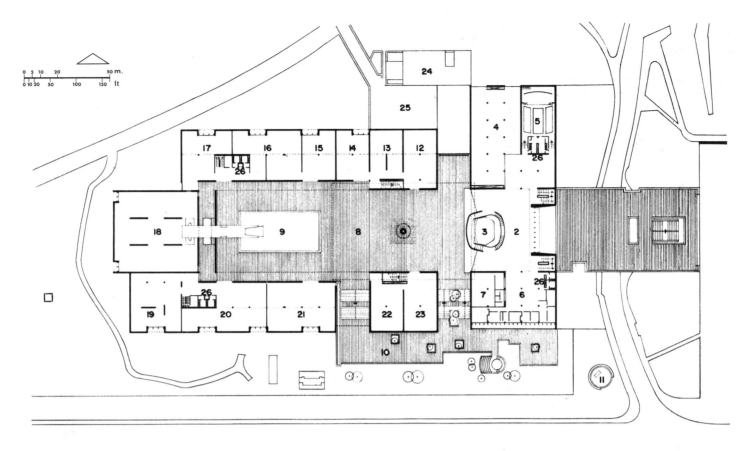

Plan of main floor of the museum: 1. Main entrance; 2. Lobby; 3. Orientation Room: Presentation of Mexican Anthropology; 4. Temporary exhibits; 5. Auditorium; 6. Information, shops, cloakroom; 7. Books; 8. Inner court, or patio; 9. Pool; 10. Outer court; 11. Tlaloc monolith; 12. Exhibit: Introduction to Anthropology; 13. Mesoamerican Room; 14. Exhibit: New World Origins and Mexican Pre-history; 15. Pre-Classic Archaeology; 16. Archaeology of Teotihuacán; 17. Toltec Archaeology; 18. Mexica (Aztec) Archaeology; 19. Archaeology of Oaxaca; 20. Archaeology of the Gulf of Mexico; 21. Mayan Archaeology; 22. Archaeology of Northern Mexico; 23. Archaeology of Western Mexico; 24. Machine room; 25. Courtyard and parking area; 26. Toilets.

Plan of upper floor of the museum: 1. School of Anthropology; 2. Library; 3. Book collection; 4. Reading room; 5. Exhibit: Introduction to Ethnography; 6. Cora-Huichol Ethnography; 7. Purepecha Ethnography; 8. Otomi-Pame Ethnography; 9. Ethnography of the Sierra de Puebla; 10. Ethnography of Oaxaca; 11. Ethnography of the Gulf of Mexico; 12. Mayan Ethnography; 13. Ethnography of Northwestern Mexico; 14. Social Ethnography; 15. Connecting gallery; 16. Toilets.

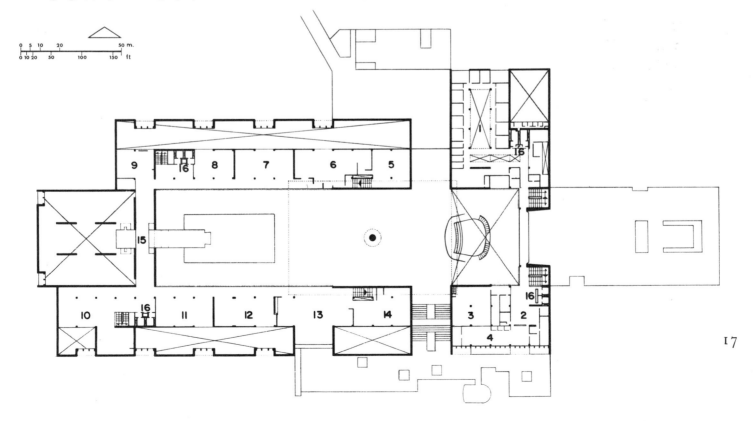

17

Construction of the new National Museum of Anthropology began in February 1963. Chapultepec Park, in Mexico City, was chosen as its site in order to make the Museum easily accessible to Mexicans and foreign visitors alike. The park has been a recreation area since Aztec times. Various construction techniques and artistic devices, primitive and traditional as well as

shows a considered relation between open spaces and the surrounding environment. Perhaps more than any other part, its sports installations (especially the stadium) are integrated into the landscape as felicitously as were the pre-Hispanic constructions.

Architectural use of color and texture also arises from the character of the landscape and from the builder's sensitivity to intrinsic qualities of materials taken from the natural environment. The Indian builders with great feeling recognized and utilized the possibilities of light intensity in their compositions. In this way they enhanced color and texture to a degree that these became not accessory values but harmonious elements of structure in themselves—as can clearly be seen in the powerful sculpture of the Temple of Quetzalcóatl in Teotihuacán, the Xochicalco reliefs and the compositions of the main pyramid of El Tajín, or in any Mayan architecture. Work conceived from such premises enriches the landscape an   at the same time blends with it unobtrusively.

In colonial architecture, natural qualities of color and texture are similarly treated as is evident in examples at Ocotlán, San Francisco Acatepec and Teziutlán, and even in the varied and marvelous combinations of limestone and tezontle (a reddish volcanic stone) used in innumerable buildings in Mexico City built during the colonial period. Among contemporary buildings, the University City attempts to revive the use of these native constants of tradition in its large murals, which (notwithstanding their uneven quality) demonstrate the continuing importance of color and texture in architecture.

Now, as before, geology provides us with the same fundamental building materials, and even though new methods may make it possible to use them more advantageously, primitive techniques and implements still survive in many areas and for special purposes. For this reason, some plastic continuity ensues from the handwork of the artisan in his use of such traditional processes. Technical boldness should be recognized as another constant in the tradition of Mexican architecture. Ornamentation in pre-Hispanic Mayan architecture is not limited to a cautious harmony with its environment but also provides lessons in building techniques that are still applicable. Ashlar (i.e., dresses or facing) masonry, whether recessed or projecting, was treated as an independent structural element that, when joined to the rest, not only finished a design but added to the stability of the whole. To translate these observations into a more

modern, were combined in the building, both for aesthetic and for economic reasons. The imposing project was directed by the architect Pedro Ramírez Vázquez, assisted by Rafael Mijares, Pedro Campuzano and a corps of 42 engineers and 54 architects who supervised a large force of artisans and laborers working under the greatest pressure to finish the project in record time.

modern idiom, one might also say that the Mayas developed a prefabricated decorative overlay, an advanced process that doubtless required quite sophisticated planning in design and production. It would be impossible to explain the precisely executed and marvelously intricate ornamentation of Mayan architecture without assuming that the builders must have had some pre-set design and a system of mass production involving precision-methods of assembly and fabrication. Such likelihood of mass production implies, moreover, the existence of a highly skilled labor force and a disciplined social organization with great respect for technical achievement and supervision. Manifest in the purity and profusion of Mayan ornamentation and in the imposing scale of pre-Hispanic building complexes, is the unity of an era and a group-imagination of constructive boldness. This was true as well during the three centuries of colonial enterprise, when some fifteen thousand religious buildings were erected—an average, that is, of one a week.

When Mexico became an independent nation in the nineteenth century, the development of architecture was initially limited because of prolonged domestic and foreign strife. With the social movement of 1910, however, the Mexican people renewed their ties with the cultural past of their land, and when peace returned after the Revolution and its constructive stage began, there was a revival of the basic constants of tradition described above. Unquestionably, these have provided a vital lesson for contemporary architects: that technology dedicated to the service of man, infused with an overriding respect for man and a love of nature, is an essential precondition for valid architectural creation. This is not to say, however, that the architect should seek to express himself in archaic formulas. His respect for cultural tradition should be shown, instead, by preserving its values through original and organic solutions in which landscape, contemporary technology and cultural tradition are all wisely considered in answering the human needs of his own age. The foregoing observations were all taken into account in the architectural planning of the National Museum of Anthropology.

The first concern of the project was the creation of a scientific museum to serve an educational purpose and a broad public. Such were the considerations in selecting its site, in arranging its interior space and auxiliary services, and especially in defining standards for the realization of the museographical aspects of the project. The site chosen was a broad expanse of Chapultepec Park, the most beautiful natural park in Mexico

City, regularly visited by the largest and socially most varied percentage not only of the city's but of the nation's population. This lovely and accessible site ensured that the museum would have an immediate cultural impact as well as a long tradition since it was a recreation area for the Aztec emperors themselves.

In order to finish the construction, moving, and installation in the allotted nineteen months, authority was centralised in the office of a project director, who co-ordinated the recommendations of forty scientific consultants, sponsored special archaeological and ethnographic surveys, arranged for the transportation of large archaeological pieces from various regions of the country, supervised the transfer of the entire contents of the old museum, ordered the classification and cataloguing of the entire contents of the museum with electronic equipment, directed museograpie installations, trained a large staff of bilingual guides and issued commemorative medals and publications. All these tasks were carried out simultaneously with the building of the Museum and preparation of the museographic sections. The total budget for all these activities and for the construction task itself was $ 14,000,000.

Fundamentally, the layout of the museum can be reduced to a single rectangle running from the outer courtyard to the Mexica Room. The entrance plaza, intended as an informal and completely open approach is indicated only by paving and is framed by natural vegetation. This open area leads directly to a lobby of the same width—roofed and delimited on four sides, however—where the public is received, oriented and then channeled to the individual exhibits. This modular width and the same materials are continued out into the patio, where the seemingly floating cover of the huge umbrella roof gives the visitor a different sensation, for although this area is only partially enclosed, he definitely feels that he is inside the museum. At the other end of the courtyard is the largest and most important exhibition hall, The Mexica Room, characterized by a strongly ceremonial air that causes an immediate respectful response. Here, too, the same width is maintained and the same materials are employed: gray floors, Santo Tomas marble, white marble, aluminium and glass.

The lobby not only serves to channel the public on to the educational and general services, but it also provides a place for receptions, ceremonies and an introduction to the museum. For this social purpose, in addition, an official chamber and a dais for ceremonies and receptions were provided on an upper level. On a lower level is the Orientation Room in which, with moving models and audio-visual devices, a summary of the entire scope of pre-Hispanic cultures covered in the museum's twenty-five rooms of exhibits is offered to the public. The aim of encouraging a casual and fluid circulation by the public, of giving it free access to the rooms either in the consecutive manner of a tour or by individual visit according to personal preference, led to the conception of a central nucleus of distribution created in the form of a courtyard or esplanade, which on account of its magnitude might have become a patio. An intermediate solution, known as the quadrangle layout, was borrowed from classical Mayan architecture. It consists of a kind of patio bounded by enclosed buildings that communicate with the outside by means of clear spans of their corners and through doorways, arranged in register between galleries, thus maintaining a sense of the exterior merging with the interior.

Essentially, the central patio is made up of two zones that are differentiated by the light they receive. One area, covered by the umbrella, contrasts with the other section which is open and has a pool connected to the Mexica Room, thus recalling the lake origins of that culture and also emphasizing the principal chamber of the museum. In order to enhance the feeling of spaciousness and permit free circulation at all times in this essentially outdoor area, it was desirable that part of the patio be covered, especially because of the annual rainy season. Therefore, borrowing from man's practice of shielding himself from the elements, the designer used an umbrella-like form to protect the space. This type of roof, because of the possibility of extra elevation over the adjacent wall surfaces, leaves an open strip above the masses arranged around the space, creating the impression of a protected courtyard. Also, since the museum is situated amid the luxuriant vegetation of Chapultepec Park, it was feared that the rain run-off would be blocked by fallen leaves and would result in an uncompensated load on the umbrella roof. To eliminate this possibility a circular area concentric with the column was opened in the roof to allow the rainwater to

The great dedication and strenuous effort of the Mexican worker made possible the rapid construction of the museum. The contemporary Mexican inherits a long tradition of workmanship, as evidenced in the sacred cities of Teotihuacán or Tula in the central highlands, Monte Albán in the state of Oaxaca, or Palenque in Yucatán. Although the most up to date architectural, engineering and structural means were used to build the new museum, many pre-Hispanic techniques were still utilised by the workers. The pride of workmanship, guided by a communal goal, has given a unique character to the edifice. (*Above*): the manual treatment of volcanic stone called *recito*, filled the patio area with the echoes of ancient ways of building. (*Below*): during the building of the Museum the men worked, ate and slept at the site. At night, when the sounds of work had died down, dozens of camp-fires would appear, and the men would have their supper, now as in the pre-Hispanic past, made up of *tortillas*, rice, beans and an occasional piece of meat.

The scaffolding for the main steel structure of the umbrella was set in place before starting work on other parts of the museum, in order to permit unobstructed movement of the bulky construction machinery. The reinforcing frame was then covered with wood and filled with poured concrete to create this huge supporting member. (*Right*): cables were later extended from the uppermost segment of the column (viewed from the roof, to the left), thereby providing a single central suspension point for the umbrella roof. With an area of about 265 by 175 feet, this constitutes the largest roof in the entire world supported by one column.

(*Below*) after the massive walls of the main museum spaces were erected they were faced with plaques of Santo Tomas marble brought from Puebla in order to integrate architectural color and texture with the park environment.

drain off freely. Furthermore, to make this practical necessity into an ornamental feature and to call attention to it, a continually running stream of water was introduced in the form of a gentle, veil-like waterfall. A mixed structural solution was dictated by the relatively short time available for completion of the entire project. The part of the building containing the lobby, auditorium, library, school of anthropology, children's installations and general offices had to be built with a prefabricated steel framework that could easily be assembled after the central umbrella and the exhibit section were finished. This was necessary because the heavy machinery used to construct the umbrella required more movement, and also because it was essential that the exhibit rooms be ready as early as possible in view of the complexity of the museographic installations. The architectural program of the main portion is a two-story structure enclosing a spacious central patio. In the interest of saving time, the

Overleaf:
A curtain of water falls from the vast umbrella roof, veiling the central support column—in fact a monumental fountain—and then drains off through the pavement. The sculptor Chávez Morado has represented major events of Mexican history in bronze relief.

(*Above*): the view from the Mexica Room shows the gigantic umbrella roof extending over half the patio, thus offering protected access to the adjoining exhibition rooms during the rainy season. (*Left*) A graceful sweep of glass, aluminium, and marble forms the exit from the vestibule to the central patio. An Aztec inscription on the marble above relates the pilgrimage of the Chichimec Indians and the founding of the Aztec capital on the site of present-day Mexico City. (*Below*): in the unroofed area of the inner court, the ochre hued pool, with its natural lake vegetation, recalls the legendary origins of the Aztec culture at Atzlán in western Mexico. At night a symbolic fire is lighted in a ceremonial brazier placed in front of the sculptured conch that is used to sound the hour. The four primal elements of air, fire, earth and water are thus introduced into the setting.

two-level interiors surrounding the courtyard were constructed with prefabricated girders made up of three plates; columns were made of welded four-plate sections (all welded joints were X-rayed, either in the plant or on the building-site). The spanning elements of the lobby part of the two-story section rest on trusses about ten feet high, articulated at their ends to accept possible seismic movement as well as their permanent load, and to avoid transmission of vertical stress to the supporting columns, which had to be slender both for spatial and aesthetic considerations.

Since the prime purpose of the museum was educational, various psychological factors had to be considered in the creation of interior and exterior space. The very generous interior spaces were dictated by the need to provide an atmosphere in which the visitor, in spite of crowds, would be able to enjoy a suitable degree of privacy and repose for contemplating the museum displays in a leisurely and rewarding way. To avoid the fatigue commonly produced by a large museum, exhibits were also placed in the gardens adjacent to each room, and circulation patterns were arranged in such a way as to prevent the visitor from passing through more than two display rooms without entering the patio (on the ground floor) or at least looking down on it (on the upper floor). This intermittent change of atmosphere has a restful effect and is a constant reminder that the museum is in a park. The first-floor exhibition rooms have ceilings of two levels. The low-ceilinged portion of each room serves as an introductory section in which background data and a summary of the exhibit are presented; the other section, double in height, makes it possible to use striking large-scale displays to dramatize the cultural achievements of a particular epoch.

All the necessary adjuncts of a museum with a scientific and a dynamic educational mission have been provided. These include nearly twenty thousand square feet of workshops, laboratories, store-rooms and research offices; a temporary exhibition hall of sixty thousand square feet; an auditorium seating three hundred and fifty persons, equipped with stage film and simultaneous-translation equipment; the National Anthropology Library consisting of a quarter of a million volumes; the National School of Anthropology, with accomodation for five hundred students; provisions for school children, including a projection room, studios for drawing and for work models, an outdoor theater and a play area, besides a cafeteria and restaurant for four hundred persons.

The continuing exploration and research into Mexico's pre-Hispanic past being conducted throughout the country requires that the museographic layouts be flexible enough to be adapted to new finds whenever necessary. For this reason, abundant electric outlets were installed in the walls, spaced only six feet apart, and ten-foot radial units were set in the floors. Unlimited potential for illumination was provided in the ceilings through modular units that can be combined to meet any requirement. The entire exhibition area, measuring nearly a hundred thousand square feet, which linearly represents an electric circuit of more than three miles, is furnished with air-conditioning and air-filtering mechanisms, fire and burglar-alarm systems, radio broadcasting equipment and provisions for future installation of audio-visual presentations in each exhibit hall.

The museographic conception was meant to provide a scientifically exact presentation which at the same time would be visually so effective that a museum visit might constitute a true dramatic spectacle and experience. Because the prime concern was to bring the cultural message of the museum to all its visitors, the architectural aim was not merely to create a space with the usual structural elements of floors, walls and ceiling, which would provide adequate quarters for observing the pieces comfortably, but also to create the means of preserving and displaying these properly, to awaken and enhance the observers' interest and enjoyment and to elicit some emotional response before the relic or work of art. Construction of this building required the utmost in technical resources and innovation.

◄ The second floor of the museum is enclosed with a striking geometric grill that is reminiscent of ancient Mayan ornamentation, suggesting a modern version of a schematized serpent. The play of light and shadow across this repeated motif furnishes a vivid contrast to the plain, bold treatment of the ground floor, where only the entrances to the various rooms are emphasized.

The gardens adjoining the exhibition rooms contain live examples of the vegetation indigenous to each region. Here, as outdoor complements to some of the oldest artefacts on display in the New World Origins and Mexican Pre-history Room, is a landscape of trees and shrubs, some of them prehistoric, from one of the most ancient settled sectors of the Valley of Mexico.

The opening of interior spaces to the outside, a characteristically Mayan architectural solution, is enriched here by linking the courtyard ▶ level with that of the school facilities and restaurant by means of a broad stairway. Following pre-Hispanic tradition, the trees of the park were left undisturbed, and thus were made an organic part of the building.

A giant Olmec head awaits installation. In order to facilitate their placement, heavy monoliths such as this monumental head were brought to their assigned display rooms in the museum before the museographic installations were prepared.

II. THE INSTALLATION OF THE MUSEUM

ARCHEOLOGICAL RESEARCH

The creation of the National Museum of Anthropology has given important impetus to the development of anthropology in Mexico. Not only was a magnificent and functional edifice provided to house its collections, but researchers soon found in it a stimulus to complete vital projects which lack of opportunity, proper facilities or the necessary integration of related areas of inquiry had long kept in abeyance. The strong interest and unremitting moral and financial support of the government decisively determined the broad scope and success of the work carried out.

A general re-examination of prevailing concepts and conclusions, many of them based upon inadequate research, was essential to the proper planning of all the archaeological and ethnographic rooms. In order to present a unified vision of the development of pre-Columbian and modern Indian cultures, it was necessary to correlate the findings and criteria of the most authoritative archaeologists and ethnographers specializing in the various areas of Mexico. Only after study and discussion was it possible to reach a common consensus on such basic problems as the terminology and chronology of the various stages of pre-Hispanic cultures as well as the determination of their relationship at the present time.

In conjunction with such ground-work, the Museum's Executive Council assigned to specialists the preparation of a series of monographs that would bring together all the knowledge available on each archaeological or ethnographic area. These studies, together with the contribution of museographers and educational specialists, were used to plan the exhibition rooms. The detailed monographs—some three thousand pages of original research—constituted a virtual encyclopedia of Mexican anthropology.

Field surveys for collecting background data and materials necessary for the ethnographic exhibits were also successfully undertaken. The haphazard system of the old museum was so extreme that the only ethnographic collections lay in the storerooms of the former building. The necessity of collecting more accurate material was even more pressing in view of the speed with which traditional patterns of Indian culture are being modified by modern ways of life.

In less than eight months, seventy ethnographic expeditions covered the country. These forays, directed by specialists for particular rooms, included a museographer, a photographer and assistants. Thus, thousands of carefully catalogued domestic and ceremonial objects from all over the country reached the museum. These expeditions, producing more than fifteen thousand photographs, hundreds of drawings, tape recordings of Indian music and languages, films, and a mass of observations, gathered for the museum a vast research-file of incalculable value for future ethnography.

The archaeological collections already on hand were among the richest in the world; nevertheless, many new pieces were acquired for the new Museum, on a scale and within a time without precedent. Special excavations were sponsored in the Mayan cemetery of Jaína (Campeche), where nearly four hundred burials with funerary offerings of the highest scientific and aesthetic value were found. A permanent camp was built on the site to provide facilities for future work and proper supervision of this find.

Hundreds of pieces became the museum's—and the nation's—property, through donation or by purchase of private collections. The famed collection of Miguel Covarrubias, perhaps the choicest privately assembled sampling of pre-Hispanic art ever made in Mexico, was acquired *in toto*. Some four thousand pieces, representing all the pre-Columbian cultures, were also acquired from the Spratling, Navarrete, Field, Pepper, Hedlung, Villanueva, Leof, Kamffer, Juárez, Frias, Corona and Hecht collections. There are in these recently acquired collections several objects recognized throughout the world as masterpieces of pre-Columbian creativity. One of these, the Olmec image of an athlete commonly known as "The Wrestler," is unquestionably one of the finest examples of Mexican archaeological art. Unusually important monumental sculptures from remote parts of the country, where they had lain for centuries, often without proper safeguards for their preservation, were also acquired by elaborate means. The giant monolith of Tlaloc, the rain god, undoubtedly the largest archaeological sculpture in the hemisphere, was brought from the village of Coatlinchán, about thirty miles from Mexico City. Almost twenty-five feet tall, this monolith is estimated to weigh about one hundred and seventy tons. Because the carving is not complete, it is difficult to identify the image as Tlaloc's. But certain details of the face—the strange perforated nose-plug—and the general aspect of the figure, suggest a water deity, either Tlaloc or Chalchiuhtlicue. The fact that it was found in the dry bed of a stream appears to support this hypothesis. Besides, its unquestionable stylistic similarity to a water goddess found at Teotihuacán carved from the same type of stone clearly marks the image of the rain god as a Teotihuacán work and places it somewhere between the third and seventh centuries A.D. The transportation of Tlaloc represented one of the most ambitious archaeological undertakings ever attempted in the Americas, comparable only to the moving of "Cleopatra's Needle" from Egypt to the banks of the Thames in London.

MUSEOGRAPHY

The building of the Museum and its innovatory policies have given museography a new significance. Museography might be defined as the methods used in presenting the contents of a museum to facilitate the visitor's understanding and appreciation of them. A comprehensive and scientific exhibit of the Indian past and present of Mexico was the result. Archaeological techniques were used to unlock the heritage of the past, the methods of ethnology were applied to the study of the present. The aim was not merely to show some particular facet of a group—magnificent as this might be—but to offer the broadest integration of its cultural aspects. Each exhibit is an array of related aspects: geographic environment, means of subsistence, working techniques and trade practices, forms of daily and communal life, historical development and cultural attainments in science and learning as well as religious practices and beliefs. Art has a central role in the exhibits, but only because art is the recurrent element of a people's vitality and the most faithful reflection of its culture's social, political and economic aspects.

To fulfill the museum's educational and scientific mission, the collaboration and supervision of educational and anthropological advisers as well as construction experts was secured. Consultants included physical and social anthropologists, linguists, historians and ethnographers assisted by specialists in geology, botany, paleobotany, paleontology and other related fields. Ways of reaching all levels of the public were studied, down to details including the form and even typography of the explanatory notes.

Still another contribution to museography by the new institution is that objects are not abstractly shown. Explanatory aids, archaeological and ethnographic material graphically relate the object to the community that created it. Generous and imaginative use is made of audio-visual aids. A group of ceremonial objects, the uses and meanings of which are difficult to understand by physical appearance alone, is explained by depicting the rites in which they are used. Elements of architecture, city layouts, popular dwellings, when too fragmentary or unavailable, have been reproduced in models large enough to convey a clear idea of their original disposition and general aspect. This is the case of the sizable outdoor model of Teotihuacán, segments of the Temple of Quetzalcóatl, the *Danzantes* of Monte Albán, details of the palaces of Mitla and, perhaps most notably, the murals of the Temple of Bonampak and the main palace of Hochob. Dioramas effectively project hunting scenes, forms of trade, handicrafts, and religious

Above left :

During the Classic period (6th-9th century A.D.) the island of Jaína in Campeche was a Mayan cemetery. Excavations undertaken by a team of archaeologists and physical anthropologists uncovered 400 graves during a three-month expedition concurrent with the building of the museum. In the foreground is a direct burial in semi-flexed position; in the background, an urn into which the bodies of dead children were placed.

Above right :

In the Mayan hall of the museum is a reconstructed grave showing the two principal positions for human burials at Jaína: flexed in a sitting position or extended.

Below right :

A fetal burial beneath an overturned clay bowl was accompanied by many jadeite beads and two figurines.

Thirty miles from Mexico City, in the little village of Coat-linchán (meaning "in the home of the snake"), a pre-Hispanic rain god lay sleeping for centuries in a dry stream bed *(above)*. The sculpture's scale and general appearance gave support to its identity as Tlaloc, the principal pre-Columbian rain god whose image was venerated in several forms throughout Mesoamerica. After a year's preparation, involving hundreds of people, Pedro Ramírez Vázquez supervised the transport of the huge statue to the site of the new museum. He is seen making the arrangements with engineers Alonso Cue and Valle Prieto and archaeologists Aveleyra and De Robina *(center left)*. The giant statue was raised by cables, in order to be placed on an especially built trailer for transportation to the capital *(below left)*. The local inhabitants, however, were determined to keep the statue, since superstition held that if Tlaloc were removed, the rains—and thus life itself—would cease. During the night, the local inhabitants cut the wires and sabotaged the trailer. To avoid further resistance, federal forces were called in, delicate negociations carried on, and the age-old struggle between tradition and change was resolved. The leader of the village *(lower right)* addressed his people, assuring them that Tlaloc would be pleased in his new home, and persuaded them to let him leave on his long journey.

At 6 A.M. on April 16, 1964, the journey of the god began. The people of Coatlinchán watched this national treasure leave its centuries old home. In return, the village requested of the government a road, a school, a medical center and electricity, all of which have since been received. It was night when Tlaloc arrived in Mexico City *(below)*; yet twenty-five thousand people awaited him in the Zocalo. The city was prepared as if for a fiesta; lights were on everywhere, traffic was stopped and the streets were thronged. Ironically, the arrival of the rain god was greeted by the heaviest storm ever recorded for this ordinarily dry season, and there seems to have been an abundance of showers ever since.

rites, such as the Cha-Chaac ceremony, that would otherwise be difficult to convey objectively. Maps, charts, drawings contribute to the description of geographical zones, culture areas, chronological systems and development processes. In some cases, as when an archaeological piece is connected with a particularly complex cosmological concept, recorded commentary is provided.

The first floor of the museum is devoted to introductory rooms and the archaeological exhibits of the great Mesoamerican cultures. Since pre-Columbian Mexico was inhabited by a large number of distinct civilizations, an Orientation Room furnishes visitors with a general introduction to the entire collection. On entering, the visitor finds himself before a broad, curved wall surface, totally devoid of exhibits. The Orientation Room is darkened and speakers convey introductory remarks. On the screen a series of color slides are projected—scale models, diorama reconstructions, replicas of the great monoliths—synchronized with an explanatory lecture. Careful consideration is given to dramatic effect and surprise value in this fifteen-minute talk, in which the spectator sees, in rough chronological order and in area relationship, more than forty vivid scenes synthesizing Mexico's pre-Columbian life and culture, from the first perilous migration to the American continent up until the full flowering of man in Toltec culture. In order to facilitate the transition from general to specific exhibits, an Introductory Room shows the aims of anthropology itself, with concrete examples that give a panoramic view of its various branches as these yield a picture of man's evolution and culture. This enables the spectator to consider in proper perspective the particular developments and accomplishments shown in other rooms. Thus, the Prehistory Room shows the first sedentary cultures, whose effort created the first works and traditions of the subsequent Mesoamerican civilizations. Overriding the tendency of the specialist to emphasize cultural differences, the Mesoamerican Room shows those elements which cultures had in common, their evolution within particular environments and the cultural elements that were passed down intact, modified by or lost in time. The room also shows how cultures with both affinities and contradictory elements coexisted and interacted with one another, inspite of wars and other rivalries. Hereafter, the visitor is prepared to appreciate the domain of the Central Highlands represented by Teotihuacán and the accomplishments of its heirs, the Toltecs. The Aztec civilization, since it is the best known and the source of some of the most impressive works in the museum, constitutes the largest and central exhibit. The cultures of Oaxaca, Veracruz, the Mayan area, and of western and northern Mexico are presented, unlike the others, regionally. But in any case, each exhibit is ordered by a chronological sequence, from the most ancient to the most recent, permitting the visitor clarity of perspective.

On the second floor, the rooms for ethnology are located, wherever possible, directly above the corresponding rooms for archaeology on the ground floor. Thus, the ethnography of Oaxaca is directly above the archaeology for the same area. But a rigorous correspondence was not always possible; a number of archaeological exhibits do not have an ethnological counterpart; also, a number of living, present-day cultures have no sufficiently established archaeological past.

The subject of the first room on the second floor is an introduction to ethnography, which fulfills the same purpose for contemporary Indian cultures as does the Mesoamerican Room for their past. Social anthropology, the subject of the final room, defines the continuity between past and present Indian cultures and, at the same time, shows their cultural contribution to colonial and modern Mexico. Eight ethnographic rooms are occupied by about fifty exhibits of contemporary Indian groups, most of whose materials have never been shown before. Here, too, area or cultural affinities group the exhibits: for reasons of ecology, the Mayas are divided into two large exhibit groups, the lowland and the highland Maya, and the Indians of northern Mexico as well as those of Oaxaca are gathered into separate exhibits: other groups are shown in their natural concentration.

From the preceding remarks, one conclusion may fairly be made: perhaps nothing shows better the organic character of the museum than the fact that it is as much a museum of art as it is a museum of science, of anthropology, that a visit to its halls is as much an experience in pleasure as it is an experience in learning, that, in short, it is a museum of Mexico as much as it is a museum for the world.

It was decided to furnish the Teotihuacán room of the new museum with something that was not on view in the smaller Teotihuacán museum outside Mexico City: a full-scale replica of the first three segments of the Temple of Quetzalcóatl, with its wealth of sculpture directly reproduced by means of molds and in the original polychrome. Numerous photographs of the Teotihuacán frescoes, rich in floral and plant motifs, accompany this exhibit.

For the first time in museographic history, the inhabitants of various regions to be represented were asked to build their own habitats within a museum. Here, a Huichol chief, carrying a briefcase, discusses details of installation with museographers.

The Indians built their characteristic huts and made and installed their exhibits in the museum galleries. Here a group of Indians from the southern Pacific coast construct their characteristic dwellings. The women made typical pottery, and even the children made toy animals for the displays. The various groups brought their clothing, implements and also magical objects. Thus, with as much authenticity as possible, their ancient and rapidly disappearing cultures were recreated in the materials, forms and styles natural to them, to be preserved within the modern and wholly appropriate National Museum of Anthropology.

Mathias Goeritz comments on the close relationship between his own artistic contribution and Indian crafts: "My wall decorations in the Cora-Huichol Room are not intended to be 'works of art,' but rather are creations subordinate to the architectural environment... they celebrate Indian craftsmanship... [in] contemporary plastic terms. The use of rope for these screens was adapted from the symbolic imagery of the Huichol Indians. The colors were kept in subdued natural tones."

A Huichol from the Maya highlands packs down a straw roof set up to protect his corn harvest. The Huichols, who mostly live in the northwestern part of Jalisco, are a timid people who base their economy principally on agriculture. They are extremely religious, and they also build huts for religious purposes. These are erected in sacred caves, and offerings are placed inside.

During construction, the central patio of the museum was filled with raw materials brought from all over the country to reconstruct the native habitats in the ethnographic rooms. Cane grass *(chinamite)*, for example, was brought from the Morelos Valley for use in fabricating a full-size Nahua corn crib.

The dominant museographic purpose of the new museum was to recreate, as accurately as possible, the past and present civilizations of Mexico. Reconstructions of the great Mesoamerican temples were built in the gardens, statuary was transported from great distances to Mexico City, landscaping was conceived to enhance the various cultures, and materials were brought in from all parts of the Republic to ensure the greatest possible authenticity to the exhibits. In the exhibition rooms themselves, decoration was organically used to recreate the atmosphere of the civilization or Indian group on view. Thus, for example, large-scale wall surfaces received the spontaneous embellishment of the traditional folk-artist. In the ethnographic exhibition rooms, Indian laborers from each of the major areas of the country built with their own hands exact reproductions of their dwellings, household articles and other everyday instruments of life and work, thus offering the visitor an image of the natural *ambiance* and customs of the Indian communities.

Outside the Maya Room, workmen from Yucatán, using traditional techniques, reconstruct the imposing Mayan Temple of Hochob with stone brought from the Yucatán Peninsula.

Component elements for the museographic installations were made in workshops set up in adjacent areas that were later to become gardens. Outstanding students and teachers of the National School of Sculpture created the figures for the dioramas and models. Directors and scientific advisers maintained constant control over the work in progress in order to ensure the utmost accuracy. Costumes and implements of all sorts were exactingly copied from ancient codices and other authentic sources representative of the Indians of ancient Mexico. The artists here are sculpting the small figures to be used in the remarkable diorama of Tlatelolco seen from different angles on the opposite page.

Opposite :

One of the most spectacular museographic creations in the new museum is the diorama of the market *(tianquiztli)* of Tlatelolco. Reproduced with the greatest possible fidelity, it measures about 30 by 12 feet in area. Tlatelolco, an island near Tenochtitlán, was settled soon after 1325 by a dissident group of Aztecs. They maintained their independence until 1473, when they were subjugated by Tenochtitlán. This market's wealth, variety and organization amazed the conquerors. Animals, seeds, fruits, pottery, clothing, jewelry, featherwork and many other products of the region, as well as goods brought by commercial travelers from distant places were displayed and sold. The market had its own overseers to prevent theft and other abuses.

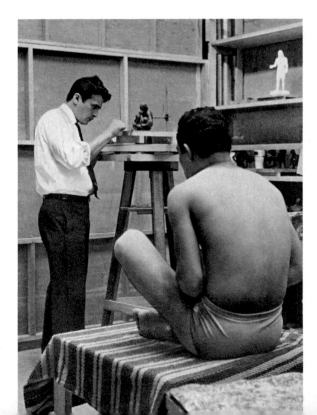

▲ Carlos Merida's abstract decoration in bright reds, yellows and blacks, illuminated from the rear, reflects the colors of the Huichol Indians.

Mathias Goeritz used *ixtle* rope, a commodity basic to the economy of
▼ the Cora-Huichol Indians, to make abstract wall decorations.

Pablo O'Higgins painted the valleys of the Purepechas, the moun-
▼ tains of the Tarahumaras and the legends of ancient western Mexico.

González Camarena's mural-backdrop for the Introduction to Anthropology exhibit shows the gradual fusion of all peoples toward a single universal race, or *mestizaje*. ▼

José Chávez Morado created the mural in the Mesoamer- ▲
ican Room and the reliefs on the patio's central column.

For the main lobby of the museum, Rufino Tamayo contributed an allegorical mural of Quetzalcóatl struggling with Tezcatlipoca, which he has explained as follows: "The fact that the concept of the struggle between good and evil was of such importance in the pre-Columbian cultures led me to think that development of this theme of duality, through the representation of the philosophical essence of those cultures, would be most fitting for a mural in the National Museum of Anthropology. It is well known that there are two hero deities in pre-Columbian mythology who clearly symbolize two forces in an unceasing contention, whose outcome determines human nature. Thus, Quetzalcóatl, or the feathered serpent, god of all good attributes, such as wisdom, light, prudence, uprightness—in short, all positive qualities—is in direct opposition to Tezcatlipoca, the god who appears in pre-Columbian mythology as a tiger and represents everything negative, such as darkness, ignorance and evil. These two figures are locked in battle against a background of day on Quetzalcóatl's side and night on Tezcatlipoca's".

◄ Mexico's leading contemporary artists created striking graphic expressions of thematic programs planned by scholarly advisers. Although the artistic quality of these works was of great importance, a prime concern was to integrate the decoration with the contents of the various rooms, in order to fulfill the fundamental educational purpose of the museum.

Carved fossil bone of Tequixquiac, Valley of Mexico. Upper Pleistocene hunting culture, prehistoric period. Approximately eight thousand years ago, this llama bone was carved by prehistoric man. It is the oldest known work of art in our continent, and the first creative testimony of Mesoamerican culture after ages of darkness.

III.

THE MUSEUM'S EXHIBITS

INTRODUCTION TO ANTHROPOLOGY ROOM

To illustrate the place of ancient and contemporary indigenous cultures in modern Mexican life the Museum of Anthropology begins its exhibits with a display that explains how the various branches of anthropology work to produce an integrated understanding of man. The exhibit hall is divided into five main sections. The first, devoted to physical anthropology, uses fossil remains to show man's origin and evolution, his place in the animal kingdom, and his relation to the other primates. The laws of genetics are demonstrated—for example, the inheritance of blood groups—along with ways in which this kind of knowledge can be applied to such other sciences as medicine and public health.

The work of the archaeologist is presented in the next section. His instruments are exhibited, and the ways in which he establishes the relationships of the objects he recovers are demonstrated. By means of the science of stratigraphy, the great evolutionary steps of human culture—the beginnings of agriculture, ceramics, weaving, and metallurgy—are placed in chronological order. Objects from Mesopotamia, China, the Indus Valley, Egypt, Mesoamerica, and South America ane offered as illustrations.

The section devoted to ethnology shows the ways in which the ethnologist studies cultures. Aspects of economy, technology, religion, art, and science are illustrated with artefacts, including objects made by the Bushmen, Masai, Haida, Hopi, and Eskimos. To demonstrate the universality of certain human concepts, objects used by various groups in the practice of magic and religion are displayed.

The section dealing with linguistics illustrates how man's many languages are studied and explains various systems of human communication—music, writing, and nonverbal methods. Lastly, a section is devoted to various applications of anthropology, such as the reconstruction of "lost cities," the study of ancient history, the preparation of primers for illiterate groups, and programs for public health and community development in backward areas.

The richly varied exhibits of the museum become cohesive when the visitor understands what anthropology is and how it works to enlarge man's knowledge of himself. The word "anthropology" combines the Greek words for " man" and "study." This "study of man" is one of the social sciences, but it is related to such natural sciences as biology. The difference between anthropology and other social sciences—sociology, psychology, and political science—lies in the anthropologist's cross-cultural approach to social phenomena. He seeks to pinpoint the similarities and differences between men by employing a comparative method. Nearly all modern social sciences investigate contemporary human beings, usually members of the great cultures of Western civilization, but the anthropologist concentrates his research on "primitive" or "preliterate" peoples, many of whom co-exist with the great cultures. He probes the origins and preliterate development of man, studying the vestiges of cultures that have often left no written history. Through this study he can establish a perspective of time and space from which to describe and understand the physical, cultural, and social aspects of the cultures he investigates. Anthropology is thus a fascinating scientific adventure, one that seeks out the similarities and differences between men.

The word "culture" is central to the language of anthropology, and many attempts have been made to define it. Culture is, most simply, inherited social tradition; it comprises those modifications observable in nature that are caused by human actions, not by natural phenomena. The divisions of anthropology are shown in the chart below. They are those customarily employed today in the United States and Mexico.

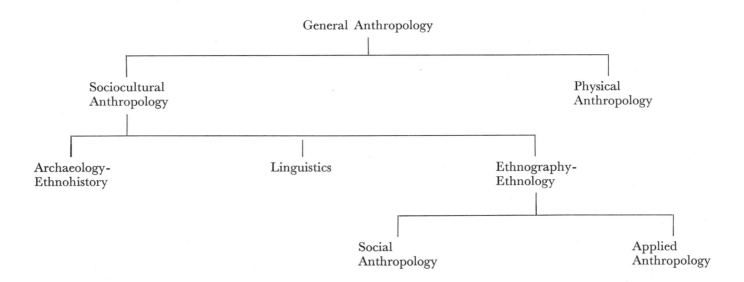

Each area of anthropology is related to the discipline as a whole. Physical anthropology, based on and intimately linked with the natural sciences, studies man as a biological entity. It seeks primarily to identify relationships between man's biological and cultural characteristics. Sociocultural anthropology studies the characteristics and implications of man's societies and cultures. Society and culture are closely linked, for any society or any organized group of people differs from other societies by its cultural or ethnic characteristics, or by both. Archaeology (from the Greek words for "ancient" and "study") is largely concerned with studying the material vestiges of peoples, not their written histories, which often do not exist. Archaeology is closely linked with ethnohistory (from the Greek words "people" and "narration" or "explanation"), which investigates the culture and society, including any written history, of a people at a certain historical moment.

Ethnography (from the Greek words for "people" and "description") studies existing human groups and describes their culture, customs, behavior, and characteristic forms of life. Thus, the ethnography of the Maya of the Yucatán Peninsula of Mexico is the detailed description of the system of life of this group. Ethnology is closely associated with ethnography and uses its data to analyze the historical development of cultures and the differences, similarities, and relations between them. The anthropologist often investigates cultures that use languages never before studied. Language is a cultural element and the instrument of expression of a people, and the need to study it has created a specific area of research— linguistics. The linguist investigates the origin and development of a language, and its relationship to the thinking and attitudes of those who speak it.

Social anthropology and applied anthropology are recent subdivisions of ethnology. Social anthropology investigates the relationship of human conduct to culture. As the physical anthropologist investigates the relationships between culture and man's physical aspect, so the social anthropologist seeks to relate man's conduct and development. In a wider sense, he makes generalizations about culture, society, and personality. This specialization has developed largely during the last fifty years. Applied anthropology, which uses the theoretical results of sociocultural studies in solving various problems confronting contemporary human groups, is also a recent development. It has assumed increasing importance in connection with induced social change, a process of identifying the internal dynamic factors of a society, causing two distinct cultures to make contact, and predicting the consequences and changes.

The Introduction to Anthropology Room is intended to acquaint the visitor with the methods and aims of this science, for which the varieties and levels of historical development of Mexico's native cultures provide an ideal laboratory for study. The room presents the study of man as a universal phenomenon, setting forth basic similarities among all groups engaged in the millennial struggle for survival, and gradually striving toward higher stages of culture. The room also provides the visitor with a general perspective for the whole Museum by differentiating the various branches of the science of anthropology.

The basic cultural features of pre-Hispanic America and their iner-relationships are presented in the Mesoamerican Room, which is decorated with a large mural painted by José Chávez Morado. Symbolically, it traces the development of Mesoamerican culture during the pre-Classic, Classic and post-Classic periods. The artist's own words explain the mural: "The earth is symbolized by a large female figure from which men evolve, changing from nomads to hunters and eventually to sedentary farmers. Part of the drama of these events is represented by propitiatory dances and other magic rites. In the center of the mural a gigantic pyramid, Man, lifting his face to the starry sky, represents the cultural achievements of the Classic period. A great stone structure emerging from the lake landscape of Tenochtitlán, symbolizes the city-state of the Aztecs. War, commerce, ritual and cultural advancement are emphasized among the dominant activities of the post-Classic period, immediately preceding the Spanish Conquest."

MESOAMERICAN ROOM

The Mesoamerican Room provides a general initiation into the cultures exhibited throughout the museum. Its displays document the main contribution of Mexico's pre-Columbian groups, their basic relationships and close interaction, their common traits, chronology and territories of development.

The northernmost border of Mesoamerican culture extends from the Soto de la Marina River (Tamaulipas) in the east to the Sinaloa River in the west. The Motagua River in Honduras and the Lempa River in El Salvador establish the southern border of this culture. The Teotihuacán, Maya, Huastec, Zapotec, Aztec and Tarascan were among the many distinctive civilizations that flourished in the area.

In agriculture, these groups practiced a system of seasonal flood-water cultivation, terracing, floating gardens and canal irrigation. They had copper tools, stone axes, planting sticks, stone and wooden hoes, and made use of granaries. Maize, squash, chili, beans, avocados, chicle, amaranth, cacao, tobacco, cotton, chia, maguey, sunflowers, rubber plants and many other products native to the Americas supplied food, medicine, clothing and had many other uses. The pre-Columbian Indian groups hunted, fished, and gathered food. They used the *atlatl* (dart thrower), the bow and arrow, and javelin in hunting for duck, armadillo, wild bear, turtle and many other animals. Hooks and lines, nets and dugout canoes were used in catching fish that were sometimes stunned with poisons extracted from plants.

The Indians clothed themselves with fur and animal hides decorated with the feathers of rare birds. The fibers of cotton, yucca, hemp and maguey were woven and made into kilts, loincloths, sandals, shawls, skirts, blankets, capes, turbans, hats, belts, headdresses and other articles of clothing. Household implements and appurtenances included bone and copper needles, awls, looms, dyes, baskets and mats. For beautification and distinction the Mesoamericans generally deformed their skulls, filed their teeth, perforated their noses, lips and earlobes, painted their faces and bodies, dyed their hair or shaved their heads, used various methods to achieve strabismus and tattooed themselves. They adorned themselves with ear, nose and lip plugs, breastplates, necklaces, bracelets, ankle bangles, rings, masks and other ornaments made from jade, rock-crystal, obsidian, amber, turquoise, clay, shell, gold and silver.

Each group created and developed a highly individual style of pottery. Tlatilco was outstanding for its zoomorphic pottery and figurines; Teotihuacán, for fine orange ware and frescoed pottery decoration; the Mayas, for beautiful polychrome vessels and molded figurines; the Zapotecs, for magnificent urn effigies of the gods; the Mixtecs, for fine ceramics painted in the style of their codices and the cultures of Colima, Nayarit, and the Gulf Coast for varied pottery specialties.

The social and political organization of the pre-Columbian groups was a graduated pyramid. Lords, nobles, priests and artisans were on the top and middle levels, while farmers, bearers, slaves and others occupied the lowest level. All groups placed much emphasis on knowledge of the calendar, astronomical observations, systems of numbers and writing, medicine, architecture and the preparation of chronicle codices as well as on crafts such as metallurgy, lapidary work, shell, and bone carving. The architectonic style of temple foundations developed from the simple platform of the Cerro del Tepalcate to the elaborate twin temples of the Aztecs, embellished with magnificent murals at Mul Chic, Teotihuacán, Tamuín and Tizatlán. This same style was elsewhere adapted in beautifully decorated vases. The religion of the Mesoamericans was embodied in a polytheistic pantheon. Their gods were related to natural phenomena, the earth and other elements, as well as to death, war and the underworld. Although names varied for different cultures, the gods had the same attributes, purposes, colors and cardinal directions over which they presided. Death was of primary concern. Sometimes cremated, bodies were generally buried, according to the individual's social rank. The poor were interred in holes, along with offerings of food, jewels, weapons, tools and other belongings. Important personages were buried in tombs with rich offerings. As in other cultures, there was a strong belief in an afterlife, in which these provisions would be useful. In brief, Mesoamerica developed from a hunting and gathering culture to that varied and splendid order of civilizations the Spaniards confronted in the sixteenth century.

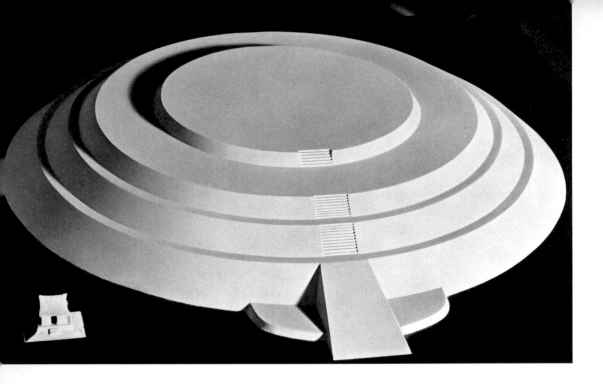

One of the most characteristic features of Mesoamerican pre-Columbian cultures are the so-called "pyramids"—in reality, stepped platforms of varying heights and forms that were built as bases for a rather small temple placed at their summit. These structures, which have a long architectural development in Mesoamerica, are completely different in purpose from Egyptian pyramids, which invariably served as tombs. Essentially, New World pyramids served for the scientific purposes of astronomical observation and chronological recording, for communal religious celebrations, for the making of war or the declaration of peace. They were also the setting for huge civic rituals involving music, dance, poetry and sports. Particularly among the Aztecs, they were the scene of human sacrifices.

Pyramid, Cuicuilco. Upper pre-Classic period, 8th-3rd century B.C.

Pyramid of the Sun, Teotihuacán (State of Mexico): Teotihuacán culture, Early Classic period, 3rd century B.C.-5th century A.D. For scale comparison, the model is set alongside models of two Mayan temples: one of the principal temples at Tikal, Guatemala (Classic period, 4th-7th century A.D.) and the Temple of the Cross, Palenque, Chiapas (Classic period, 5th century A.D.).

Pyramid, Cholula (Puebla). Cholula culture, 9th - 5th century B.C. A white outline drawn over a photomural of the site of the Cholula pyramid indicates its original position and that of the present Catholic church built in place of the original Indian temple. The foreground model shows the many successive substructures that were built from the middle of the pre-Classic period through the post-Classic period of Teotihuacán.

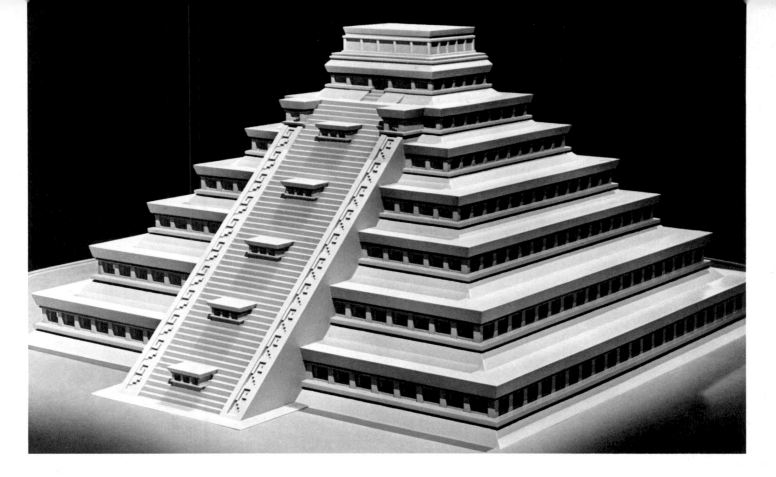

Pyramid of the Niches, El Tajín (Veracruz). El Tajín culture, 6th - 8th century A.D. This model reproduces one of the most celebrated pre-Hispanic structures. The superimposed rectangular terraces are covered with niches and windows.

Principal pyramid of Tenochtitlán (Federal District): Aztec culture, 14th-16th century A.D. This pyramid, facing the setting of the sun, was enlarged and remodelled eight times. The temples upon the platform were dedicated to the god of rain and the god of war.

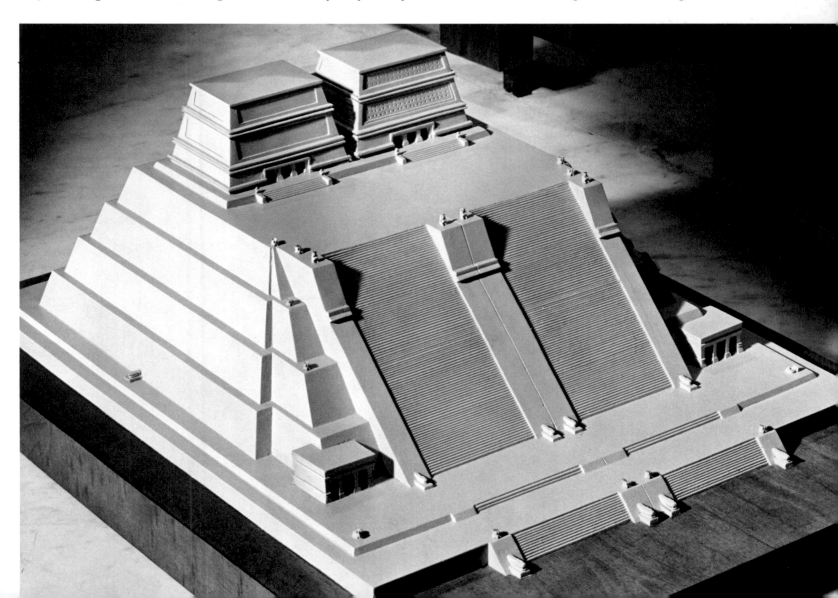

NEW WORLD ORIGINS AND MEXICAN PREHISTORY ROOM

The discoveries so far made about the most ancient cultures found in Mexico help to explain more fully their geography and chronology within the context of general prehistory in the New World and also aid in establishing the origins of American man. To show what we know of his appearance, life and environment is the object of this room.

The most important discoveries of the earliest presence of man in Mexico were made in the valleys of the central highlands. Proof has been found of a primitive culture dating from about 15,000 to 7,000 B.C. These groups, the direct descendants of the first Siberian immigrants to North America, were nomadic hunters and gatherers of wild plants. Their clothing and sustenance depended on the hunting of large mammals, such as the mammoth, bison, horse and various American camels. They led a transitory life, either in small caves or natural rock shelters or, when in open areas, built temporary shelters of a framework of branches covered with grass or animal skins. They cooked and probably kept domesticated dogs. They did not as yet know how to fire clay to make pottery, and their technology was limited to chipping and pressure-flaking of hard stone to make implements and weapons. Their culture, in short, is comparable to Europe's Upper Paleolithic Age of some twenty-five thousand years ago.

In 1947, near Tepexpán, northeast of Mexico City, fossil remains were found of one such primitive hunter, known as Tepexpán Man. His bones lay in sedimentary clay, deposited at the bottom of a large lake that covered the basin of the central highlands during the late Pleistocene period. In 1952 and again in 1954, archaeologists obtained new material that completed the knowledge derived from the Tepexpán find. In Santa Isabel Iztapán, less than two miles from Tepexpán, two mammoth skeletons were found in the same geological stratum. Between their bones were lodged points and blades of chipped stone, such as prehistoric man used to kill and dismember his quarry.

The region of Tequixquiac, in the north of the Valley of Mexico, is also of prime importance in the country's earliest prehistory. The bones of extinct fauna and crude stone instruments found there indicate the presence of man at least twelve to fifteen thousand years ago. The site also yielded an exceptional sculpture, carved from the sacrum of a llama. It is evidence that man had attained sufficient ability to produce not only utilitarian artefacts, but also art. Probably the oldest example of art in the New World, it is a worthy prelude to the magnificent artistic flowering of later Mesoamerica.

In time, culture underwent continuous transformation. With the disappearance some eight thousand years ago of the great mammals of the Pleistocene period, the hunters gradually ceased their nomadic existence and began to attach themselves to the land, gathering wild seeds and grasses. Dependence on land led to a discovery of the greatest transcendence: the development of agriculture, based on cultivation and controlled utilization of edible plants. Agriculture gave life sufficient safety, continuity and organization to allow man the development of his creative and civilizing activities for the first time.

The principal crop of ancient Mexico, the foundation of the whole economy and the crucial food of the aboriginal cultures, was maize (Indian corn). To determine its botanical origin, the region of its domestication, and the antiquity at which it appeared, still remain preoccupations for scholars and scientists. Recent excavations in Coxcatlán (Puebla) give evidence that it was here that corn was transformed by man from its ancestral wild form into a domesticated plant, sometime between 5,200 and 3,400 B.C.

Beginning with a difficult, even hostile environment, Mesoamerican man, through his creative capacity and effort, proceded to build the foundations of an indigenous culture, the intellectual and artistic achievements of which were to astonish, millennia later, its European conquerors.

Primitive man lived in North America as long ago as some 1,500 to 7,000 years before the Christian era. He was a nomadic hunter who ▶ fought against gigantic animals, such as those represented at the rear of the New World Origins and Mexican pre-History Room, and he used the beast's meat, bones and hide to aid him in his own survival. In the foreground is a reconstruction of a pit found in 1954 at Santa Isabel Iztapán, which yielded both the fossil remains of a mammoth and the stone points and knives that brought it down.

The struggle of primitive man against giant beasts is scientifically recreated in this scene of the killing of a mammoth at Santa Isabel Iztapán. At this time, Meso-american man was at a transition point between a nomadic and a sedentary culture.

This full-scale replica of the excavation site of the fossil mammoth at Iztapán, along with the stone and metal implements used in the kill, are proof of man's earliest struggle for survival against great odds in the New World ten to twelve thousand years ago.

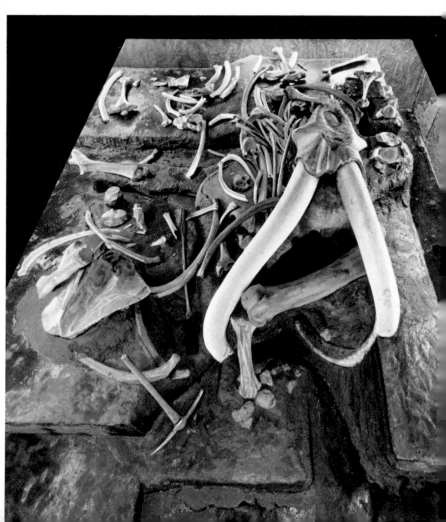

The mandible, or jawbone, of an Imperial Mammoth (Archidiskodon Imperator) found in the Valley of Mexico. Upper Pleistocene, eight to twelve thousand years old.

The carapace, or shell, of a glyptodont (huge armadillo) found in the region of Tequixquiac (Valley of Mexico). Upper Pleistocene, approximately twelve thousand years old.

Exhibit in the New World Origins and Mexican pre-History Room showing several fossil remains of Upper Pleistocene fauna, corresponding to mammals which, together with primitive man, were the first to inhabit the Valley of Mexico.

Terra-cotta bottle in the form of an acrobat or contortionist, from Tlatilco (Federal District): height, ca. 10 ½ in. Pre-Classic culture of central Mexico, 12th - 8th century B.C. The Tlatilco potters rendered in clay many representations of their people, their everyday activities and the dancers and acrobats who probably played an important social role. This water bottle is of fired red clay, and one of the figure's up-raised legs serves as a spout.

PRE-CLASSIC ART AND ARCHAEOLOGY OF CENTRAL MEXICO

Let there be light!
Let it dawn in the heavens and on earth!
There will be neither glory nor grandeur
Until the human creature comes.
Until man is formed.

POPUL VUH.

The pre-Classic (or formative) cultures that flourished in the Central Plateau—an area comprising the present-day states of Mexico, Puebla, Morelos and Tlaxcala—originated in village settlements which began the development of agriculture at least two thousand years before the Christian Era. There are three main periods of historical-cultural evolution: Early, Middle and Late (or Upper) pre-Classic.

For hundreds of years, groups of nomadic hunters and food gatherers moved about Mexico from one region to another, settling from Tamaulipas to Puebla and Chiapas. In these places they found wild food plants, such as agave, maize, squash, chili pepper, beans, amaranth and cactus. With time and after observing the germination of some of these plants, the nomads progressed from food gathering to a settled agriculture, which led to further cultural advances.

Agriculture obliged man to remain in a certain place, permitted him some degree of control over his food supply and gave him time to develop crafts and begin to ponder the mysteries of the world around him. Thus is was possible for him to form the first villages, to organize his life in a single place. In line with this new sedentary tendency there developed huts for shelter, cults of the dead, pottery making and weaving and the other cultural advances that characterized the peoples of the formative or pre-Classic Age.

The crafts of the people of that period were pottery making and the modeling of figurines. They also produced various artefacts and utensils, such as scrapers, projectile points, bone awls, deer-horn polishers and volcanic rock tools for grinding corn. Pottery was mainly of a domestic type, finished in black, white and reddish-brown pigments. The smooth surface was decorated with very fine incising and at times rubbed with cinnabar. The figurines were modeled by hand, with clay-pellet appliqué features, and often represented women; probably a link with certain fertility cults.

During the Middle pre-Classic period (1300-800 B.C.) some settlements became more elaborate as the result of greater demographic concentration, and huts were built on an earthen platform faced with stones or slabs. This innovation can be regarded as the birth of architecture in Mexico. In this period, also, the settlements in the Basin of Mexico increased, with new villages at Copilco, Tlapacoya, Coatepec and Atoto. In addition, sites in Morelos such as Gualupita and Chalcatzingo were occupied, along with various places in Puebla, Ajalpán and Las Rocas.

About 1300 B.C. the Olmecs of the Gulf Coast began penetrating into Puebla, Morelos and the Basin of Mexico. They introduced a more advanced culture, which influenced the people of the highlands, and thus constituted true civilizing colonies. The Olmecs brought with them magic cults related to agriculture, the concept of a society governed by magicians or sorcerers, the cult of a jaguar god related to rain, rituals such as the ball game and music and dance. They also introduced wooden or clay masks representing animals and human beings, as well as pyrite mirrors and jadework.

During this period the people utilized serpentine hatchets and hoes to work in the fields, bone awls and needles for sewing and chisels and drills for wood carving. They used vegetable fibers such as cotton, yucca and agave and eventually developed true textile arts. They traded in raw materials such as jade, shell, kaolin, serpentine and turquoise—commodities often obtained from distant places.

The dress of these groups consisted of kilt-like skirts and breechcloths, short capes and belts, turbans and hats, sandals, leather jackets, and ornate headdresses, chin straps and facial bindings. They adorned themselves with necklaces, earplugs, bracelets, mirror-like chest plates, and bangles made of clay, shell, jadeite, pyrite and other materials. In general, custom dictated that the people deform their heads from birth, mutilate their teeth, paint and tattoo their bodies, shave their heads completely or partially and perforate the nasal septum and earlobes to accommodate decorative plugs.

Pottery of the Middle pre-Classic period attained maximum quality when craftsmen created beautiful forms such as stirrup-handled bottles, vases decorated with jaguar motifs, animal and plant-shaped vessels made from kaolin, plates with pouring spouts and bowls. They also developed new decorative methods, such as the cameo technique, fresco or dry-stucco painting, thumbnail marking, rocker stamping and grooving. Figurines continued to be modeled by hand, but incisions and punchings were added, principally to represent the eyes and mouth. True minor sculpture was created, such as representations of ballplayers, acrobats, musicians, dancers, masked sorcerers and dwarfs. Most notable were the beautiful hollow, generally large "baby-face" figurines, usually white or cream-colored and depicted in a sitting position. They clearly demonstrate the artistry which Olmec potters brought to the Valley of Mexico.

During the Late pre-Classic period (800-200 B.C.), the Basin of Mexico became quite densely populated. Much the same population increase occurred in the states of Morelos, Puebla and Tlaxcala. Among some groups during this period—especially the Olmecs of the Gulf Coast and Oaxaca—terracing was practiced in agriculture, crafts and barter were augmented, astronomical observations were initiated and a system of hieroglyphic writing was developed, as was a number system with which a calendar was made. Formal construction was also undertaken, including such projects as bases for temples, observatories and systems of irrigation canals. With the appearance of the first temple bases, small ceremonial centers were also formed. From these, the growing priestly class governed those around them and directed the worship of various deities, which began to be represented with recognizable attributes: Huehueteotl, the "old god" and a god of fire, appeared in the form of an old man with a brazier on his back, and an early guise of Tlaloc, the future rain god, also sprung forth.

Perhaps the most distinctive trait of this period was the initiation of religious architecture, evidenced by the above-mentioned stepped bases for temples, as found at Cerro del Tepalcate, Cuicuilco and Tlapacoya. The temple form underwent a discernible process of development at these sites, but its culmination was to come many years later at Teotihuacán. Pre-Classic architecture had its rudimentary origins in the hut or shed on a raised platform, as seen in the Middle pre-Classic period. At Cerro del Tepalcate, in the State of Mexico, a three-step platform was subsequently built and faced with stone, upon which was erected a temple-hut made of mud and saplings with a thatched, pitched roof. Over the years, these platforms grew in height and area as the old temple-huts were burned to make way for new edifices.

At Cuicuilco, on the outskirts of Mexico City, the first temple bases were made of mud and had several superimposed circular platforms; but later an inclined pyramid was built there, with stone facing and a ramp and staircase to reach the upper part, where a circular mud-and-sapling temple was built over an altar. This stepped base also underwent successive modifications. A stepped pyramidal base was built at Tlapacoya, in the State of Mexico, resembling an inclined wall faced with stone, but it was smaller in scale than similar examples at Teotihuacán. Here also staircases with narrow ramps alongside were built, and stucco was used as a facing material. Three tombs in the form of stone caskets with slab roofs were found within this base. This type of burial seems to be another characteristic practice that began in the late pre-Classic period. Thus, the pyramid at Cuicuilco was the origin of the Mesoamerican religious and sacrificial structure, while that of Tlapacoya was the first formal burial site of pre-Classic America. Both had far-reaching consequences.

In summary, the cultural advances achieved during the pre-Classic, or formative, era provided the foundation for the development of the classic civilizations of the central highlands, the prime example of which is that of Teotihuacán.

The pottery of the pre-Classic peoples inhabiting villages around Lake Texcoco evidences the tradition of the central highlands and also some Olmec influence. There are bottles with stirrup handles, kaolin jars, vases with fresco decoration, vessels in the shape of whistles and aquatic animals, and many other decorative types. A few are seen here. (*Upper left*) Jar in the shape of an armadillo, from Tlatilco (Federal District): height, ca. 9 ½ in. Middle pre-Classic period, 12th - 7th century B.C. (*Upper right*) Bowl in the shape of a fish, with Olmec carving, from Tlatilco (Federal District): height, ca. 5 ½ in. Middle pre-Classic period, 12th - 7th century B.C. (*Lower left*) Polychrome goblet from Chupicuaro (Guanajuato): height, ca. 8 in. Upper pre-Classic period, 5th - 2nd century B.C. (*Lower right*) Three handled jug from Tlapacoya (State of Mexico): height, ca. 5 in. Upper pre-Classic period, 7th - 3rd century B.C.

Huehueteotl, the old god of fire, from Cuicuilco (Federal District): height, ca. 7 in. *(left)* and 5 in. *(right)*. Upper pre-Classic period, 6th - 2nd century B.C. Both of these anthropomorphic braziers are images of one of the earliest deities of Mexico.

Hollow clay figures showing Olmec influence, from central Mexico: height, ca. 16 in. *(right)* and ca. 11¾ in. *(left)*. Middle pre-Classic ▶ period, 12th-7th century B.C. The seated "babyface" figurines, usually white or cream colored, are the most outstanding of this period,

Jar in the shape of an old man, from Tlatilco (Federal District): height, ca. 10 in. Middle pre-Classic period, 12th-7th century B.C. This extraordinary dark-brown polished clay figure of an old man sticking out his split tongue attests early man's acquaintance with physical illness and suffering.

Mask embodying the quality of life and death, from Tlatilco (Federal District): height, ca. 3½ in. Middle pre-Classic period, 12th-7th century B.C. Life and death are wedded in the face of this dramatic clay mask, that expresses a magico-religious belief in the duality of all experience.

Clay figurines from Tlatilco (Federal District): Middle pre-Classic period, 12th - 7th century B.C. (*Upper left*) Mother and child: height, ca. 4 ½ in. (*Upper right*) Masked sorcerer: height, ca. 4 in. (*Lower left*) Female symbols of duality: height, ca. 4 ½ in. (*Lower right*) Woman embracing dog: height, ca. 3 in. Detail of the head of a terra-cotta feminine figure, from Tlatelolco (State of Mexico). Hundreds of such funerary offerings were found in the Tlatilco tombs. The female figures seem to demonstrate the Nahua preference for plump hips and a feminine concern with hairdressing.

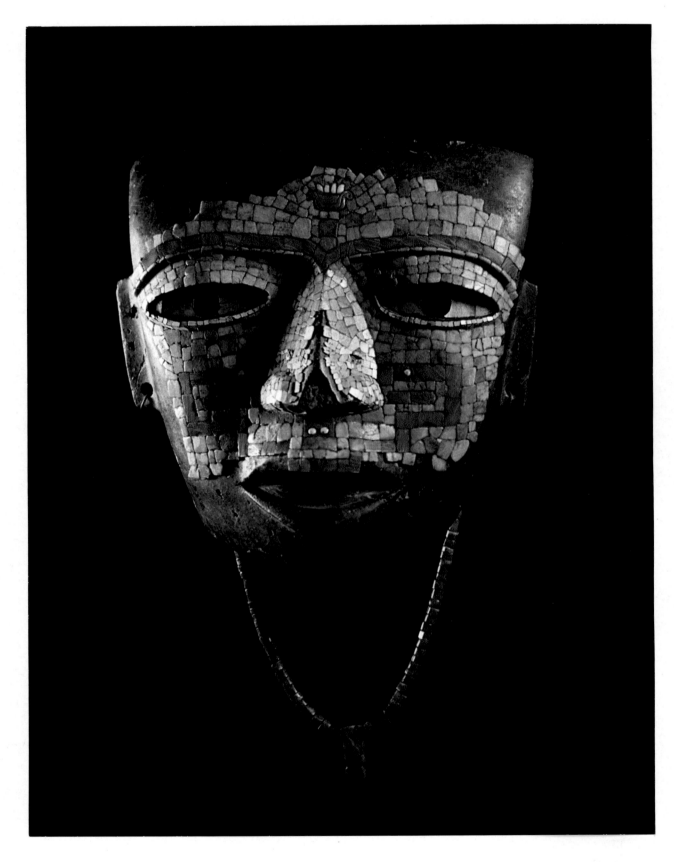

Funerary mask inlaid with turquoise, serpentine and shell mosaic, from Teotihuacán (State of Mexico): height, ca. 8½ in. Teotihuacán culture, 3rd-8th century A.D. Masks were placed on the dead bodies of these ancient people, creators of a civilization that extended to the limits of Mesoamerica. These funerary masks were also used by priests in certain ceremonies and were supposedly worn by the gods to hide their divinity.

ART AND ARCHAEOLOGY OF TEOTIHUACAN

When there was only night,
Before there was day,
Before there was light,
They gathered.
The gods met,
There in Teotihuacán.

CODEX MADRID.

The sacred city of Teotihuacán, one of the largest and most famous archaeological sites of the world, was already an enormous deserted ruin at the time of the Aztec Empire and constituted a mystery for the Aztecs themselves. Its monumental proportions, massive buildings and broad avenues, in their awesome silence and abandonment, evoked for them the mystic presence of their ancestors, whom they imagined to have been a race of giants, since only giants could have built such a colossal city.

Teotihuacán, thirty miles north-east of present-day Mexico City, was the largest political and religious center of pre-Columbian America and the capital of the great Teotihuacán culture. These people had settled principally in the valleys of the central highlands. This was, however, a civilization of extraordinary geographical extent, exerting direct influence all the way from the present states of Nayarit, Durango, Zacatecas and Chihuahua, in the northern part of Mesoamerica, to its southernmost points at the Mayan centers of Kaminalijuyu and Tikal, in Guatemala.

The Teotihuacán culture, through various periods of gradual development, endured for approximately ten centuries. Its origins may have derived, partially at least, from the evolution of the Late pre-Classic cultures about the first and second centuries B.C. Its final collapse, when the city was sacked and burned by warrior peoples who later consolidated the Toltec Empire, occurred about the middle of the eighth century A.D. In the highlands of Mexico, the Teotihuacán culture encompassed the Classic period of the development of the various Mesoamerican civilizations.

Teotihuacán owed its grandeur to the extraordinary power that its gods wielded over its people. Everything indicates that the machinery of government of the great city was in the hands of a powerful priestly class. The deities associated with water, and consequently with the harvest and fertility, occupied a prominent position in the Teotihuacán religion. The rain god Tlaloc, in particular, seems to have been all-powerful, and representations of him appear in a multitude of media and forms in Teotihuacán art. Located in a relatively arid environment, the city was wholly dependent on its water supply in order to flourish—or even to survive. Consequently, the god of rain is an omnipresent force, and Teotihuacán art is veritably obsessed with the repetition of flowers, fruits, trees, streams, drops of water, seashells, aquatic creatures and all sorts of water motifs. Appropriately, green is one of the favorite colors of the Teotihuacán artist. Among the great urban centers of antiquity, Teotihuacán provides an outstanding example of detailed city planning.

Buildings were grouped in rectangular blocks bounded by streets and avenues disposed along the length of a main central axis. Extensive and effective drainage systems further demonstrate the existence of a carefully worked-out plan, and a concern on the part of the authorities for satisfactory functioning of public services. Advanced agricultural methods allowed the Teotihuacán people to develop a flourishing economy to maintain their great city, one of the sites of Mexico's ancient grandeur.

The temples and the palaces of priests and government officials were grouped toward the center of the city. Encircling this ceremonial center were other groups of sumptuous smaller palaces, which were undoubtedly inhabited by the privileged classes. Located concentrically about the periphery, were numerous houses inhabited by what must have been the middle class of the city, consisting mainly of professionals, artisans and others engaged in various specialized occupations. In this zone, excavations have revealed information of great interest about the daily life, industry, commerce and domestic activities of the Teotihuacán culture. These people seem to have lived in *barrios* (districts), each of which was occupied by a particular group of artisans such as potters, painters, lapidary craftsmen, masons, sculptors and shell and bone carvers. Some of the *barrios* were given over to artisans who came from other parts of Mesoamerica—mainly from the Gulf Coast—and who contributed importantly to the integration of Teotihuacán culture and art with their own styles and techniques.

Finally, scattered around the great valley of Teotihuacán were countless huts and small houses built of perishable materials, hardly any vestige of which remains. These modest abodes sheltered most of the rural population, whose work in the fields provided sustenance for the city dwellers. At the peak of its splendor, Teotihuacán was probably inhabited by nearly one hundred and fifty thousand persons.

Teotihuacán art is an art of great beauty and solemnity. Its austere architecture is distinguished by an almost monotonous repetition of superimposed stepped platforms, each formed of a sloped element, or talus, in the lower part and another vertical element, framed by molding, in the upper part. The impressive proportions achieved by the combination of these elements gives Teotihuacán its grandeur, and also its originality, for no European City had a style or a landscape like Teotihuacán's.

The fundamental characteristic of Teotihuacán monumental sculpture is its architectural and functional character. Almost all known carvings from this culture were intended as decorative elements for buildings, as is the case with the astonishing statuary and reliefs adorning the façade of the so-called "Temple of Quetzalcóatl." Even in the great monolithic water deities of Coatlinchán and Teotihuacán, the angular and rigid sculptural treatment imparts a marked architectural feeling. There is also, however, the famous La Ventilla ball-court marker, a sculpture composed of four varied superimposed elements, in which the Teotihuacán artist expressed himself with extraordinary freedom. Lapidaries have left magnificent samples of their craft; their realistic funerary masks are especially noteworthy, as are a large number of figurines and ornaments carved from jadeite and other precious stones.

Teotihuacán pottery is distinguished for its simplicity and elegance of form. Highly-polished brown or red ceramics are very characteristic, and the orange clay commonly used produced light and fine-textured vessels. The most widespread forms are "tripod" cylindrical vases, bowls, and pots with three small conical supports and flared necks; basaltflange bowls; vessels bearing the effigy of the rain god Tlaloc and the small, rounded and long-necked types referred to as "flowerpots." Varied techniques were used in decorating pottery, including incising and scraping in relief, fresco painting and a laborious process of scraping and inlay similar to *cloisonné*.

Teotihuacán was, without doubt, the pre-Columbian city with the greatest and most varied display of mural painting. Using brilliant colors and advanced techniques, the Teotihuacán people decorated hundreds of square yards of the interior walls of their temples and living areas. On the exterior, mural paintings were applied to cornices and façades of buildings, stairways, patios and the stepped bases of temples. A wide range of subjects was represented: the principal benevolent deities, priests in an infinite variety of ceremonial or propitiatory attitudes, strange mythological animals, vivid naturalistic scenes and many depictions of everyday activities that provide an invaluable source of material for a better understanding of the complex philosophy and customs of this ancient civilization.

In the Nahuatl language of the Aztecs, Teotihuacán means "the place where one becomes a god", reflecting the belief that its rulers were transformed into divinities after their death. This belief is not wholly inappropriate, for if Teotihuacán's rulers could not become gods, they could and did govern a society in which religion was the shaping power of social, political and economic activity as well as of creative activity in the arts. By virtue of that social order and what it made possible in culture, Teotihuacán has been, and continues to be, the most studied of the ancient pre-Columbian cities as well as one of the most frequently visited and admired archaeological wonders of Mexico.

Model of Teotihuacán, the "city of the gods." 3rd. century B.C. - 8th. century A.D. Teotihuacán, in the Valley of Mexico, was the largest political and religious center of pre-Columbian Mesoamerica. Its most important structures are known as the Pyramid of the Sun, the largest in ancient America, and the Pyramid of the Moon. Its direct influence reached from Northern Mexico to Central America and lasted about ten centuries. Teotihuacán can be considered the first urban plan realized in the American hemisphere. Tenochtitlán, the Aztec capital, and other settlements were patterned after this city.

Hollow clay figure of Xipe Totec, god of youth and fertility. Height, ca. 4 ft. Teotihuacán culture, 7th-9th century, A.D. The skin of vic- ▶ tims sacrificed to this god was removed and donned by his priest to dramatically symbolize the yearly, springtime renewal of the earth's surface.

71

Examples of Teotihuacán culture, 3rd-8th century A.D. Sculpture in the form of a human skull: height, 28 ½ in. Huehueteotl: 25 in. Ball-game stele bearing the face of Death: ca. 4 ft. Photomural of the Pyramid of the Sun. The spiritual unity of Teotihuacán derived its tremendous force from the single-minded dedication to the gods, reflected in these different creations.

Full-scale polychrome model of a corner of the Temple of Quetzalcóatl. Teotihuacán culture, 3rd-8th century A.D. (*Foreground*) La Ventilla ball-court marker: height, ca. 7ft. Teotihuacán culture, Classic period, 6th-8th century A.D. The stepped architectural masses of this magnificent temple, perhaps the most outstanding of Mesoamerica, are covered with a profusion of carved reliefs, which were originally painted in bright colors. The ornamentation is dominated by a giant representation of Tlaloc surrounded by the heads of plumed serpents. Shells and various forms of aquatic life appear frequently in these reliefs. Since Teotihuacán was situated in a relatively arid area, water was of great importance in the life and beliefs of these ancient peoples. Flowers, fruits, streams, shells and sea or river creatures appear constantly in Teotihuacán art, and the preferred color of the style was green. The Ventilla ball-court marker standing before the temple is composed of four beautifully superimposed sculptural elements. Originally representing the eternal interplay of the heavenly bodies, the game had magical and religious connotations that were later lost, thereby converting it into a secular sport and gambling pastime. The game was called *ollama* and the playing field *tlachtli*.

74

The Plancarte Vase, made of jadeite, represents Tlaloc: height, ca. 9 ½ in. Alabaster jaguar: height, ca. 7 ¾ in., both Teotihuacán culture, 5th-8th century A.D. The rain god Tlaloc, on the left, is accompanied by the jaguar. Both deities are dominant in many different cultures of the pre-Hispanic world.

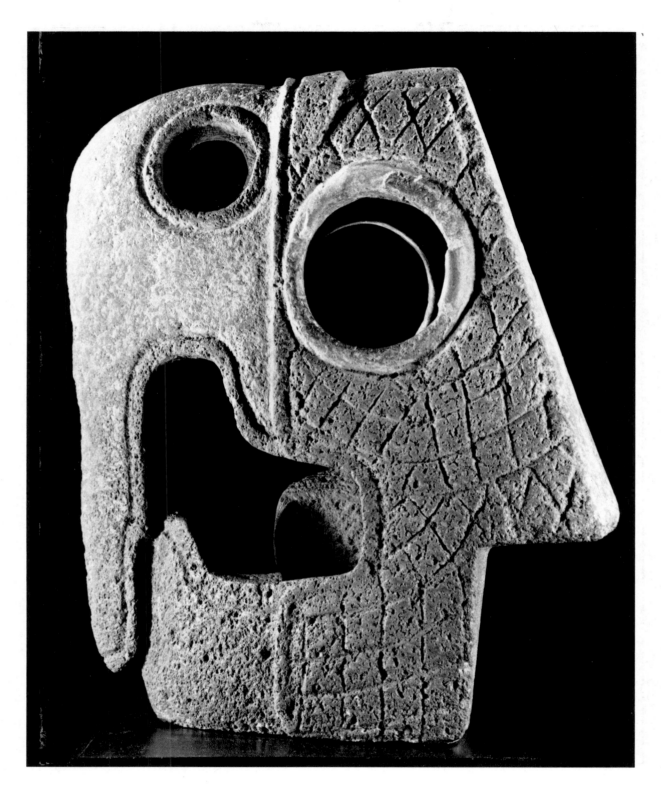

Macaw head, from Xochicalco (Morelos): height, ca. 22 in., 3rd-9th century A.D. An advanced culture based on elements borrowed from Teotihuacán flourished in Xochicalco toward the end of the Classical period. Little is known about this culture, but among its creations were extremely sophisticated zoomorphic stylizations such as this bird, in which art and nature find superb balance.

Pair of clay figures from Teotihuacán (State of Mexico): height, ca. 7 in. Late Teotihuacán culture, 7th-8th century A.D. These figures represent dwarfs adorned with plumed headdresses, ear-plugs and cotton garments that leave the abdomen and chest bare. A great variety of such small figurines was made in Teotihuacán, ranging from such realistic representations as these to nearly abstract expressions of the human figure. The decorative headdresses, elaborate ear-rings generally made from obsidian, and decorative costumes are indicative of the richness of this ancient civilization.

The Paradise of Tlaloc, reproduction of fresco from Tepantitla, (State of Mexico). Teotihuacán culture, 4th-8th century A.D. Tlaloc presides over the waters that pour down upon the earth, and rain springs from the god's hands. Behind him rises a tree heavy with fruit and blossoms, the home of richly plumed songbirds. At both sides, priests make offerings and scatter seeds over the earth made fertile by Tlaloc. Here, in eternal happiness, live those who have died by water or who were killed by storms and lightning.

Clay mask with nose and earplugs, from San Miguel Amantla, Azcapotzalco (Federal District): height, ca. 4 in. Teotihuacán culture, 5th-8th century A.D. The visage of Death is placed over the face, and the stylized butterfly, symbol of the god Quetzal-cóatl, imposes silence on this funerary mask. Funerary masks usually represent the human face in a summary but life-like form. They were offered to the dead and left in the grave, and are testimony of the role of religion in Teotihuacán culture.

One of the most characteristic and distinctive art-forms of the ancient people of Teotihuacán was the representation of the human figure and face. Human features, above all, were realized almost always with great realism, but casting a marked expression of poised dignity. All these clay faces, like those sculpted in stone for funerary masks, bear an emphatic similarity in facial characteristics. It is therefore probable that these faces represent with considerable faithfulness the most generalized physical prototype among the people of Teotihuacán.

In the first stages of Teotihuacán civilization, these human figures were freely hand-modelled. Later, during the last stage of this culture, the introduction of molds allowed more elaborate and abundant reproduction of these figurines, at the expense of individuality and artistic quality.

Red and yellow clay figure with chest opening that contains a human face, from Santiago Ahuizotle (State of Mexico): height, ca. 4 in. Teotihuacán culture, 5th-8th century A.D. This serene clay figurine has another tiny being dwelling in its breast, perhaps representing the soul or the inner self. Even as to the mediaeval Christian mind courtesy was not merely the public display of manners, but social exercise of inner grace, so this figure may express the Nahua ideal of possessing perfect heart and countenance.

Clay mask with feather decoration, from Santiago Almiz-ontia, Atzcapotzalco (State of Mexico): height, ca. 8 in. Teotihuacán culture, 5th-8th century A.D. No other topic has caused as much commentary, both foolish and wise, as the place of death in both ancient and modern Mexican thought. But the fact is that, like his descendant, the ancient Teotihuacán not only experienced but celebrated death in his art and festivals. Death was so much a part of life that the mask became almost an integral part of the man. This example has earplugs, a great feather headdress and face painting in white and black horizontal bands.

Orange tripod vessel with figures of jaguar, from Teotihuacán (State of Mexico): height, ca. 5 in. Teotihuacán culture, 5th - 8th century A.D. This example of Teotihuacán pottery, from the period when the culture was at its height, shows typically fine craftsmanship and purity of line. A jaguar figurine and an ornamental row of heads encircle the tripod vessel. As the classical period progressed, the motifs used in pottery decoration became more and more symbolical. In what relationship stood the jaguar, the central god of the Olmecs, to Anetzalcóatl, the plumed-serpent god of Teotihuacán, is under study.

Clay tripod vessel decorated with shells, from Teotihuacán (State of Mexico): height, ca. 9½ in. Teotihuacán culture, 5th-8th century A.D. Painting, relief, polish and appliqué were used to enhance these vessels. Here, pink and yellow seashells are embedded in the clay container and its lid for decorative effect. Fresco decoration was widespread, and applied not only to pottery but to walls of temples and palaces. Other materials, like obsidian, were encrusted in art objects and buildings.

Tripod vessel decorated with frescoed ceremonial scenes, from Teotihuacán (State of Mexico): height, ca. 6 in. Teotihuacán culture, 5th-8th century A.D. Fresco painting, so often found on the walls of Teotihuacán temples and palaces, was also used to ornament select examples of the ceramic art of the ancient Teotihuacáns. Finely painted in red, white and green, this cylindrical ceremonial vase depicts a priest or dignitary, in ceremonial dress, making a propitiatory offering to the gods.

Cylindrical vases with three supports may be considered as one of the most typical forms of Teotihuacán ceramic art, in the period of its greatest splendour. These pieces were manufactured with countless variants in the clay used, the form of their supports, and the rich decoration ornamenting their surfaces. The most sumptuous of these vases had covers and were decorated with elegant motifs, representing important personages, animals or abstract designs.

These ceramic forms were widely distributed throughout Mesoamerica, following the decline of Teotihuacán. For that reason, when they are found in other cultures, they are an excellent means of studying the chronological and spacial extension of Teotihuacán civilization. The typological affinity of these Teotihuacán vases with certain bronze vases from the dynastic civilizations of China has caused certain archaeological speculations presuming to establish a number of contacts between Asia and America in the pre-Hispanic age. These speculations, however, still lack sufficient foundation to be seriously entertained.

Plumbate vessel inlaid with mother-of-pearl, representing the face of a warrior emerging from the widely opened and menacing jaws of the sacred coyote, from Tula (Hidalgo): height, ca. 5 in. Toltec culture, 11th-16th century A.D.

TOLTEC ART AND ARCHAEOLOGY

They were indeed wise, those Toltecs.
They communed with their hearts.

ANONYMOUS.

The post-Classic period in the central highlands was ushered in by the Toltecs of Tula (Hidalgo). The era was characterized by the dominance of the military or warrior caste and by imperialist expansion, conquest and the collection of tribute.

In about 650 A.D. some Nahua wanderers from the Bajío of Guanajuato, filtering through Querétaro and Hidalgo as far as the central highlands, invaded the Valley of Mexico. Teotihuacán had at this time passed the zenith of its splendor and had entered into decline. Other Nahuas appear to have settled in Xochicalco (State of Morelos), thus initiating the development of a culture that adopted the architectural style, the plumed serpent and the ball game of Teotihuacán, together with influences from central Veracruz, the Maya region and Oaxaca.

Archaeological findings confirm that for the next two hundred years a people of a lower cultural level occupied, sacked and burned Teotihuacán, built primitive adobe structures, modified the courtyards and palaces of the great ceremonial center, occupied the surrounding houses, decorated tombs and dismantled stairways in order to re-use their carved stone. They appropriated Teotihuacán sculpture, objects and observances, celebrated the creation of the Fifth Sun (which implies the imposition of a new religion upon the Teotihuacáns) and made pottery of a type patterned after the red-on-brown Teotihuacán ceramics. These newcomers, in short, lived side by side with the older Teotihuacán population, imposed a new religion upon them, assimilated part of their culture and adopted the technology of their craftsmen.

Some Toltecs subsequently left Teotihuacán and moved on to Tulancingo and later to Tula, where they founded another city. There they worshipped Quetzalcóatl, god of the planet Venus, in its aspects of both morning and evening star. His priests, also named Quetzalcóatl, were believed to possess his attributes. Among the priestly overlords, Topiltzin Quetzalcóatl was very important; frequently confused with the god himself, he became a culture hero in his own right. Huemac, another important figure among these leaders, held power when the ascendancy of this ceremonial center came to an end in about 1168 A.D.

The Toltecs developed agriculture and handicrafts, promoted trade and evolved an artistic style borrowed mainly from the Teotihuacán and Mayan cultures. The first pottery of Tula, the Coyotlatelco type, consisted of plain pots, bowls and tripod plates painted red over a yellowish-brown base. This was followed by the cream-colored Mazapán ware, decorated with designs composed of wavy parallel lines made with several brushes and painted in red. Orange and black-on-orange vessels were found as well, together with trade ware from various places, which included plumbate and *cloisonné* vessels and other types of decoration. The Toltecs produced very flat mold-made figurines painted in blue, red, yellow, black and white; they also carved stone, wood, bone and other materials.

Toltec architecture followed the layout of the great ceremonial centers of the period. The Teotihuacán talus and panel were adopted in constructing the first substructures but were modified by inverting the proportions. The Toltecs took over from the Teotihuacán culture such decorative forms as the bas-relief, the serpent column and the use of descending figures of gods in an upside-down composition. At the same time, they were inspired by Mayan architectural decoration, a definite reflection of the far-reaching conquests of this military civilization during the tenth to thirteenth centuries A.D. They employed small columns, Atlantean figures, pilasters, ball courts and other characteristic features, particularly of the Puuc-Chenes period.

One example of the Toltec style of Tula is the Temple of Tlahuizcalpantecuhtli (Lord of the Dawn), decorated with bas-reliefs of coyotes, vultures, eagles and jaguars wearing collars. In the upper part of this edifice is a sanctuary with huge telamones and serpent columns supporting the lintels of the entrance, and pilasters adorned with bas-reliefs of warriors holding up the roof. On the same site is the so-called "Burned Palace," surrounded by a colonnade, with inner courts containing Chac-Mools and sculptured altars representing the divine messenger bearing a sacrificial offering to the sun. The Chac-Mool, a reclining male figure of basalt stone, is common at Chichén Itzá, and thus further documents the relationship between the Mayan and Toltec civilizations. Sidewalks are decorated with processions of priests or warriors in painted stucco and other constructions at the site are a ball court like that of Xochicalco, dwellings for the ruling class, a circular building dedicated to Ehecatl, god of the wind, and an altar decorated with skulls, called *tzompantli*. This type of altar, appearing later in the Aztec period, was a time establishing device, in which sheaves of sticks were drawn together and tied to mark the passing years.

Outstanding examples of Toltec sculpture in the round, as fine as the bas-reliefs, are the colossal Atlantean figures sixteen feet tall, made of four sections held in place by mortised joints. These figures represent warriors, each wearing a feather headdress, earplugs, butterfly pectoral, apron, sandals and belt with a clasp symbolizing the sun, and they carry a dart thrower in one hand and a bundle of darts in the other. These columns have their precedent in the large anthropomorphic supports of the north pyramid at Teotihuacán. Indicative also of the war-like spirit of Toltec society are smaller Atlantean figures in the form of warriors; flag holders in the shape of human or animal figures, used for the banner or insignia of the festivals of the month; slabs with representations of skeletons being devoured by snakes and the merlons, or crests of the buildings, in the form of cut spirals, symbolizing the wind.

In general terms, Toltec art may be considered as the logical and natural accomplishment of a military society, basically concerned with the consolidation of its political power over the ancient Teotihuacán world it had conquered. Although Toltecs attempted to assimilate quickly the elements of Teotihuacán culture, they never reached the refinement that characterised their predecessors, the builders of the great city Teotihuacán. Toltec art has something of a barbarous character, crudely grandiose, in which sculpture and stone reliefs representing warriors constitute the most essential and notable contribution. It is a typical transitional art, between the serene majesty and refinement of the art of Teotihuacán, which the Toltecs supplanted, and the sweeping strength of the Aztec artistic styles which were to come later.

With it all, two important events give particular importance to the Toltec stage of archaeology in Mexico. One of these is the appearance of metallurgy, originating at this time in Central and South America, for the making of utilitarian objects. The other is the compilation of the first narratives and genealogies of a truly factual and historical character, both of which offer the first historical dates of pre-Hispanic time in Mexico.

The twilight of Tula coincides with the arrival of the Chichimec groups, barbaric tribes from the north. Led by Xolotl and civilized by their contact with the more advanced peoples of the central highlands, the Chichimecs settled down in their newly conquered territories and founded a number of cities, the most notable of which was Texcoco. But by 1325, when Tenochtitlán was founded on one of the islands on Lake Texcoco, the more aggressive Aztecs had grown so powerful that they held control of all the central highlands and with it the legacy of Toltec civilization.

Colossal telamon warrior, from Tula (Hidalgo): height, ca. 15 ft. Toltec culture, 11th-16th century A.D. This warrior figure, made from ▶ great stone drums joined together in the center by slabs, was intended to serve as support for a roof. Armed and bearing the insignia of his rank, he guarded the principal entrance to the main temple of the Pyramid of Tlahuizcalpantecuhtli, the Lord of the House of Dawn.

Polychrome clay effigy of the rain god Tlaloc, from Tula (Hidalgo): height, ca. 8 in. Toltec culture, 11th-12th century A.D. Here Tlaloc is seen wearing his attribute of a feather mantle, which created the wind before the storm. The rain god was aided by Tlaloques, lesser gods in his service, and joyous deities charged with the shedding of water over the land. When summoned, these supernatural forces noisily broke their water jugs, producing thunder, lightning and rain.

◄ Columns of the Temple of Tlahuizcalpantecuhtli (replica), from Tula (Hidalgo): height, ca. 16 ft. Toltec culture, 11th-12th century A.D. The Toltecs carved their history and thoughts on such columns, like stone pages on which the sacred mysteries of their epic were inscribed.

The Toltecs, a barbarous and warlike people in their origin, not only had the military strength and the political ability to supplant their predecessors, the builders of Teotihuacán, but also the capacity to assimilate rapidly a number of creative streams of Teotihuacán civilization. Their efforts in this direction, however, bore fruit only to a certain extent, for it is always possible to recognize in Toltec stone sculpture the character of a warlike people, whose leading preoccupation was war and not refinement in the arts.

Very much in accord with these characteristics, the most frequent representations in Toltec statuary are warrior figures in diverse attitudes. Often painted with brilliant colors, these sculptures decorated palaces, temples and open spaces in the ceremonial center of Tula, Hidalgo, then capital of the Toltecs. *Polychrome sculpture of a warrior, from Tula (Hidalgo), (above)*: ca. 29 in. Toltec culture, 11th-12th century A.D. This small telamon stands before a reproduction of the polychrome friezes of the Temple of Tlahuizcalpantecuhtli, god of dawn. When the god-king Quetzalcóatl abandoned his people, he journeyed to his ultimate sacrifice, burning himself to ashes; but his heart remained intact and rose to the heavens, where it became the morning and evening star—our Venus. Quetzalcóatl continued to be one of the most important deities in Mesoamerica. Even as late as the period of Aztec splendor, he was considered a sort of cultural hero, a Promethean figure who taught his people new techniques and a much better way of life. *Statue of a warrior, from Tula (Hidalgo), (below)*: ca. 4 ft. Toltec culture, 11th-12th century A.D. Appearing in the familiar guise of a butterfly, Quetzalcóatl both shields the heart of a warrior and alights on his forehead to inspire his thoughts.

Opposite :

Reclining Chac-Mool and warriors, from Tula (Hidalgo): height of foreground figure, ca. 25 in. Toltec culture, 11th-12th century A.D. Warriors stand guard behind the characteristic reclining figure of a Chac-Mool, an enigmatic deity of multiple significance common to diverse Mesoamerican cultures. He was thought by some to be the god of life, and by others he was variously identified as Quetzalcóatl himself, or the procreative principle, or merely as a messenger between this world and the supernatural realm.

Coatlicue, "Goddess of the Serpent Skirt," from Tenochtitlán (State of Mexico). Aztec culture, 14th-15th century A.D. The creation of gods and men, of heaven and earth and all the symbols important to the religion and philosophy of the Aztecs, have been integrated into this solemn, harmonious sculpture.

AZTEC ART AND ARCHAEOLOGY

The fame and glory of Mexico-Tenochtitlán
Will last as long as the world lasts.

MEMORIALES DE CULHUACÁN.

The flowering of Aztec culture was the last great event in the history of pre-Columbian Mexico. For more than two hundred years before the coming of the Spaniards, the Aztecs had dominated the country both politically and culturally. The earliest references to the Aztecs belong to mythology rather than to history. A nomadic people, they had emigrated from a legendary place called Aztlán ("White Place") —which may have been located in the Guanajuato highlands—to the basin of the Central Highlands known as the Valley of Mexico. They called themselves Aztecs, after their place of origin. During their migration they passed through Tula (Hidalgo), where the Toltec culture was then nearing its end. After penetrating many locations in the Valley of Mexico, they finally settled near the hills of Chapultepec.

The Aztecs were first subjugated by the lords of Culhuacán, a neighboring Toltec kingdom. After gaining their freedom, they wandered once more from place to place until they reached an island shielded by reeds. There the prophecy of their god Huitzilopochtli was fulfilled, for on this isle they saw an eagle devouring a serpent—the sign given by the god to identify the site where they should settle—and in 1325 A.D. founded the modest village that was later to become the great Tenochtitlán.

At first the Aztec lords were subservient to neighboring Azcapotzalco; nevertheless their rulers Acamapichtli, Huitzilihuitl, and Chimalpopoca (1376-1427 A.D.) began to develop the city by establishing wards (*calpullis*) and organizing a society. Finally, the great ruler and conqueror Izcóatl (1427-1440) freed the Aztecs from the lords of Azcapotzalco.

From that moment on, Aztec civilization grew steadily to its maximum expansion and splendor, especially in the reigns of Moctezuma, Ilhuicamina, Axayácatl, Tizoc and Ahuizotl. Their great city was now known as Tenochtitlán, so named after one of their great rulers, Tenoch.

Just as Mayan culture would not have been what it was without mathematics, the Aztec would not have developed into its own characteristic form without military organization and war. Culturally, it was a society in which all the major achievements of the pre-Columbian cultures of Mexico—Olmec, Mixtec, Zapotec, Mayan, Toltec—were fused and used in new ways. It was pre-eminently a syncretic culture. But although the Aztecs came to dominate by war and conquest the largest area of Mexico they failed to establish effective military control over it. Moctezuma, Xocoyotzin, Cuitláhuac and Cuauhtémoc had consolidated the empire, but when the Spaniards arrived in 1519, they found ready allies among many of the Aztecs' subjugated peoples.

The conquest made of the Aztecs an isolated culture, and after three years of tenacious resistance, Tenochtitlán succumbed to the combined force of European arms and the aid given to the Spaniards by various tribes attempting to liberate themselves from Aztec rule.

At the zenith of Aztec culture, Tenochtitlán was connected with its suburbs by means of wide avenues: Ixtapalapa to the south, Tepeyac to the north and Tlacopán (now Tacuba) to the west. In addition to the avenues there was a network of canals for canoe traffic, pedestrian walks and paths adjoining the buildings. An aqueduct running from Chapultepec furnished fresh water to the city, and a dam kept the salt water of Lake Texcoco from contaminating the fresh water of Lakes Xochimilco and Chalco. There were also public fountains, a good drainage system and other urban facilities of importance.

(*Above*) Mural of the lake city of Tenochtitlán (State of Mexico) by Luis Covarrubias. Aztec culture, 14th-16th century A.D. (*Below*) Scale model of the great ceremonial center of Tenochtitlán. The great Aztec ceremonial center, measuring almost a thousand square feet in area, stood in the middle of an island that is the present site of Mexico City. From this base, which fell to the Spaniards in 1521, the powerful Aztecs ruled a vast empire encompassing most of the Indian nations of Mesoamerica.

The ceremonial area was in the center of the city, surrounded by a wall (*coatepantli*) decorated with huge serpents and pierced by only three avenues. Within the walls of the central compound could be seen the Great Temple, with its shrines dedicated to Tlaloc and Huitzilopochtli, the circular Temple of Quetza-cóatl, the ball court, the Altar of Skulls (*tzompantli*) and the *temalacatl*, a ring-like altar where gladiatorial sacrifices were held. In the ceremonial zone were numerous other civil and religious structures. Outside the ceremonial precinct were located the residences of nobles and officials made of masonry and set among orchards or gardens, the *tlacochcalli* (arsenal), the *cuicacalli* (house of song) and the *calmecac* and *tepoch-calli* (schools for the sons of noblemen and commoners, respectively). All these buildings formed a great urban complex that aroused the admiration of the conquering Spaniards in the sixteenth century.

The Aztecs had a mixed economy, based on agriculture, hunting, fishing and gathering of wild grain. Wars, tribute and trade allowed them to sustain a continually growing population. In agriculture they used canals for artificial irrigation and developed a system of cultivation on *chinampas*, a kind of floating garden made of woven mats, mud and tree trunks. The farming population, by all means the largest, was organized into clans, which held title to the land and parcelled it out to its members. In return, the farmers contributed a portion of their produce to support the costly military and priestly establishment. The Aztecs hunted with bows and arrows, dart launchers, snares and nets. Fishing was done with canoes, nets, spears and tridents.

From their labors the Aztecs obtained maize, beans, squash, *chia* (a type of sage), chili and various other vegetables and flowers. Their diet also included deer, wild turkey, duck, fish, turtle and prawns. The agave plant was a source of cochineal dye and pulque (an alcoholic drink made from the juice of the maguey). They also gathered insects and fish roe from the lake, wild amaranth, watercress and corn fungus.

Tribute from hundreds of conquered towns brought Tenochtitlán raw materials, food stuffs and finished commodities. They acquired some raw materials through trade and luxury products widely sought after and appreciated by the ruling class: prize fruits, exotic animals and birds, jaguar skins, quetzal feathers, gold, silver, jade, fine woven materials and blankets, tortoise shell, copal incense, medicinal balms, tobacco, honey, salt, cocoa and precious stones. The markets (*tianguis*) of Tlatelolco, Tacuba, Azcapotzalco and Tenochtitlán—visited by thousands of persons each day—played an important economic and social role. These markets had officials and guards who were in charge of keeping order, fixing prices, attending to complaints and preventing thievery. The vendors occupied fixed locations and displayed their merchan-dise in street-like rows of stalls. Barter in the market involved fruits, turkeys, iguanas, fish, frogs, fattened dogs, paper, copal, wood, honey, pulque, hides, pottery, medicinal herbs, cloth, jewels, prepared foods and drinks. All these goods were brought by local vendors or by *pochtecas*, peddlers who came to the market from distant places.

Although the Aztecs maintained their empire through military power, religion also played a vital role in their civilization. It permeated every aspect of their private and public life. The Aztec religion was polytheistic, with Huitzilopochtli at its head and, like much else in Aztec culture, it embraced local gods and deities adopted from conquered peoples. Among other gods were Tezcatlipoco (god of night), Huehueteotl (god of fire), Tlazolteotl (goddess of fertility), Xipe (god of springtime), Xochipilli (god of flowers and song), Coatlicue (an earth deity and the mother of gods and men), Tlaloc (god of rain), Quetzalcóatl (god of wind), Cihuateteo (deity of women who died in childbirth) and Mictlantecuhtili (god of death). These gods had well-defined attributes, governed specific regions of the universe, had distinctive colors and were associated with the cardinal points and the several spheres of heaven. Great celebrations were held in their honor, on dates fixed in accordance with the religious calendar two hundred and sixty days long: these feast days were accompanied by dances, music and games.

The central importance of religion and military power are reflected in the structure of Aztec society itself. Directly below the emperor-king were two sets of counsellors, the priests and the warriors, and both exerted a powerful and decisive influence on the affairs of state. Because tribute and trade were crucial to maintain this rigid, disciplined social organization, the merchant class also enjoyed special privileges. As Tenochtitlán grew in power and splendor, the skilled artisan, engineer, architect, and sculptor, also assumed a higher status. Religion and the learning of that period were in the hands of the sacerdotal class, which had its own hierarchy and special functions.

The priests were in charge of worship and ceremonies, festivities, baptisms and marriages, of predicting the future of newborn children, of sacrifices, of teaching and passing on knowledge, of mathematics, the calendar, astronomical observations, astrology, botany and herbal medicine, hieroglyphic writing, literature, poetry and architecture.

In the arts, the Aztecs left their imprint with the manufacture of codices, painted on skin or agave paper, that contained religious, calendar, historical and geographical data. They developed the art of working feathers and the carving of wood and hard materials such as obsidian, rock-crystal and alabaster. They modeled clay figurines and vessels—decorated principally in black on orange, black on cherry red, and black, white, and yellow on red—but also adopted the Mixtec polychromatic pottery with codex-like decoration. As examples of these crafts, mention should be made of the Bourbon and Florentine codices and the Registry of Tribute; the famous feather headdress of Moctezuma; the musical drums (*teponaxtle* and *huehetl*), with beautiful designs in low relief, skulls, animal figures, masks, and vases with representations of monkeys. Also noteworthy are large braziers, sculptured representations of gods, small sculptures of grasshoppers, plumed coyotes, feathered serpents and bearers—all exhibiting great technical mastery.

In reality, the Aztecs were outstanding sculptors and created a style or tradition that is reflected throughout a vast area of Mexico. They left to posterity great works of art such as the Aztec Calendar (or Sun Stone), a massive monument dedicated to four suns or cosmogenic worlds of an era prior to the Aztecs. These in turn are circled by bands of solar rays, precious stones, or *chalchihuites* flowers, hieroglyphics of the days and months and fire serpents, all indicating the cosmic order in great symbolic detail.

Other outstanding examples of Aztec carving include the images of Xiuhcoatl, the fire serpent, with his crown of stars, who led the sun in its trajectory through the celestial vaults; Ocelocuauhxicalli, a sculpture in the form of an ocelot, with a huge hollow in its back to serve as a receptacle for the hearts of those sacrificed, and the god Xochipilli, prince of flowers and deity of love, song and poetry, depicted with a mask and seated on a throne decorated with flowers and *chalchihuites*.

The most important monolith is that of Coatlicue, the earth deity and the mother of gods and men. The work owes its significance to its plastic qualities as well as to its religious symbolism. Goddess of birth and death, Coatlicue gave and took away life; she was the incarnation of this duality in all human life—two moments of a single process of experience the acceptance of which was of the outmost importance in Aztec thinking. Because she represents life-in-death and death-in-life, Coatlicue, also known as the "Goddess of the Serpent Skirt," is portrayed headless. In place of a human head, she has huge serpent heads, symbolizing the earth-bound character of human life. She has no hands; in their place are two more serpents, in the form of eagle-like claws, which are repeated at her feet. These eagle-images symbolize the sky-bound aspiration of human life and are, therefore, opposite to the earth-bound symbolism of the serpent. Hanging from her neck is a necklace of open hands alternating with human hearts. The hands symbolize the act of giving life, and the hearts, the taking of life through sacrifice to the gods in exchange for their preservation of cosmic order. In the center of the collar, in front, hangs a human skull with living eyes in its sockets and another identical one is attached to her belt. These symbolize life and death together as parts of one process. In sum, Coatlicue depicts the contradictory but necessary principles of existence: the expectation of an after-life within a natural, mortal world.

Naturalistic squash carved in diorite from Tenochtitlán (State of Mexico): height, ca. 7½ in. Aztec culture, 14th-16th century A.D. The ▶ Mexica Room presents artefacts of the civilization of the Aztecs, the last of the pre-Hispanic peoples, whose blood was merged with that of the Spanish conquerors to create the populace of modern Mexico. The immense height of the ceiling, the beautifully proportioned walls and special illumination all further the spiritual and reverent atmosphere. The squash in diorite is the same color as the vegetable. To the left is Coatlicue; at the foot of the calendar stone is a brazier from Tlatelolco and on the right is the moon goddess, Coyolxauhqui.

Monolithic serpent head, from Tenochtitlán (State of Mexico): height, ca. 3 ft. Aztec culture, 14th-16th century A.D. This colossal basalt head of the four-nosed snake (*nauyaca*) is associated with Xiuhcóatl, the "Fire Snake." Serpent sculptures like this were used to protect the enclosures of the principal temples of Tenochtitlán or were placed at the bottom of stairways.

◄ *(Far wall)* Sun Stone: diameter, ca 12 ft. *(Foreground)* Stone of Tizoc: height, ca. 34 in., diameter, ca 12 ft., from Tenochtitlán (State of Mexico). Aztec culture, 14th-16th century A.D. In the foreground of this general view of the Mexica Room is seen the round trachyte monolith known as the Stone of Tizoc, which was found in the main square of Mexico City. Its reliefs, composed of geographical and calendar glyphs, record the conquests of Tizoc. Against the walls of the Mexica Room can be seen the Sun Stone, or so-called "Aztec Calendar."

Chalchiuhtlicue, "Goddess of Surface Waters," from Tenochtitlán (State of Mexico): height, 20 in. Aztec culture, 14th-16th century A.D. Chalchiuhtlicue, wife of the rain god Tlaloc, rules over fountains, springs, rivers, lakes and all the waters on the surface of the earth. A highly beneficial deity, she appears here as a simple native woman wearing the typical *quechquemitl* that is still worn by women in many of the Indian communities of Mexico.

Most critics of pre-Hispanic art would share the conviction that the most notable Aztec achievement in the arts was in sculpture. Stone sculpture was the art of the greatest excellence among a people that knew how to project in sculpture a complex variety of ideas, beliefs, ancestral myths and religious fears that formed the world in which their civilization developed. As is natural with a religious people, the gods constituted the main subject of their art. These masterpieces were mostly recovered from the subsoil of present-day Mexico City, built upon the ruins of Tenochtitlán, the ancient Aztec capital. The styles of Aztec religious sculpture show great variety. On certain occasions, the gods appear merely as human beings, executed simply and realistically. In other instances, as with the monumental sculpture of Coatlicue, or with the goddess of the moon, stone has been the vehicle to convey an ancient symbolic and mythical tradition.

Xochipilli, the "Flower Prince" and also god of games and pleasure, from Tenochtitlán (State of Mexico): height, ca. 3ft. 9 in., including carved base. Aztec culture, 14th-16th century A.D. Also the tutelary god of spring, love, dance, poetry and theater, in this image Xochipilli wears a mask, jade earplugs, a necklace and jaguar-skin sandals, and is seated on a throne decorated with flowers and butterflies (the symbol of Quetzalcóatl). Flowers and song symbolized the Nahua pleasure in the enjoyment of beauty and art.

Diorite head of the moon goddess Coyolxauhqui, from Tenochtitlán (State of Mexico): height, ca. 30½ in. Aztec culture, 14th-16th century A.D.   The goddess Coyolxauhqui, the moon, was decapitated by her brother, Huitzilopochtli, the sun.   Both are the mythological children of Coatlicue.   In this sculpture her eyes are nearly shut, as if she were asleep.   The decorated, golden, tear-like disks on her face are related to the sun.

Coiled serpent, from Tenochtitlán (State of Mexico):
height, ca. 12½ in. Aztec culture, 14th-16th century A.D.
Aztec sculpture, which was symbolic and expressionistic
in the depiction of its deities, also created very realistic
animal and plant forms. This graceful, rhythmically
coiled serpent extending its long forked tongue, is a remarkably fine example of such naturalistic animal sculpture.

◄ Obsidian vessel in the form of a monkey, from Texcoco (State of Mexico):
height, ca. 6 in. Aztec culture, 14th-16th century A.D. A stylized
monkey, as smoothly polished as a mirror, grasps his tail in this imaginative design. The technical skill displayed in carving and polishing
this volcanic-glass vase without metal tools makes it one of the most
valuable pieces in the museum and an absolutely unique model.

Curly-haired coyote, from Tenochtitlán (State of Mexico):
height, ca. 15 in. Aztec culture, 14th-16th century A.D.
The coyote, the owl and the opossum are three animals
that appear repeatedly in Nahua myths. This coyote
image covered with curled hair—formerly believed to be
feathers—displays craftsmanship of the very highest order.

The wind god, Ehecatl, from Tenochtitlán (State of Mexico): height, ca. 16 in. Aztec culture, 14th-16th century A.D. This figure of Ehecatl, or Quetzalcóatl with his attributes of the wind god, has characteristic mouth and eye-sockets inlaid with obsidian. Ehecatl caused the winds and swept away the clouds to prepare for the coming of Tlaloc and his helpers, the Tlaloques.

Ceremonial vessel *(cuauhxicalli)* in the form of a monolithic jaguar, from Tenochtitlán (State of Mexico): height, ca. 3ft. Aztec culture, 14th-16th century A.D. This jaguar vase was hollowed at the back to serve as a repository for the hearts of human sacrificial victims. At the bottom of the circular receptacle in the jaguar's back are delicately carved symbols of Huitzilopochtli and Tezcatlipoca, whose cult was associated with the beginnings of human sacrifice.

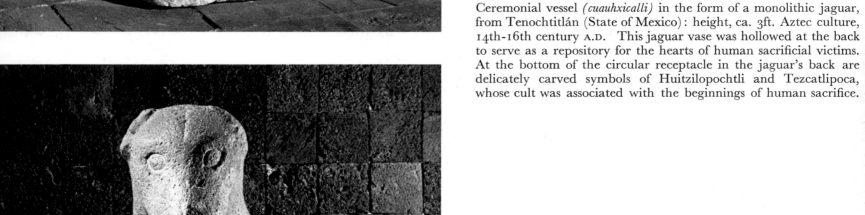

Dog, from Tenochtitlán (State of Mexico): height, ca. 23½ in. Aztec culture, 14th-16th century A.D. The *itzcuintli*, the species of edible dog depicted here, is now extinct. These animals were especially bred to be sold as delicacies at the great market of Tlatelolco.

(Left) Cihuapipiltin, "Goddess of the West," height, ca. 13 in. (Right) Coatlicue, goddess of life and death, from Tenochtitlán (State of Mexico): height, ca. 30 in. Aztec culture, 14th-16th century A.D. The fleshless face of this small representation of Coatlicue is crowned with a ring of skulls. She wears a pectoral composed of two hands flanking a skull, and a *huipil* decorated with feathers signifying great worth. The heart motifs refer to sacrifices. The goddess of the life principle is accompanied by Cihuapipiltin, another deity of death, as signified by the westerly direction of the sun.

◄ Altar of skulls *(tzompantli)*, from Tenochtitlán (State of Mexico): height, ca. 3 ft. Aztec culture, 14th-16th century A.D. Every fifty-two years, the Aztecs "tied off a century." Each year was represented by the addition of a cane until the full number of fifty-two canes were tied together into sheaves, as shown to the left of the altar. The symbolic corpse of time *(Xiuhmolpilli)* was buried through the central opening visible in the upper part of the *tzompantli*, also known as the "Tomb of Time," which was richly decorated with skulls and subdivided with friezes of many crossed bones.

Coatlicue, from Tenochtitlán (State of Mexico): height, ca. 3 ft. 9 in., Aztec culture, 14th-16th century A.D. In this representation, large tears drop from the sightless eyes of Coatlicue who otherwise wears a skirt of serpents and a funerary mask, her traditional iconography.

Images of the Cihuateteo, spirits related to death, from Tenochtitlán (State of Mexico): height, 27½ to 30½ in. Aztec culture, 14th-16th century A.D. Every woman who died in childbirth, giving birth to a warrior at the sacrifice of her own life, was

deified and included among the divine spirits known as the Cihuateteo or woman goddesses. These examples have stylized faces in the form of skulls; their hands are converted into claws, their breasts are bare and their skirts are tied with a cord.

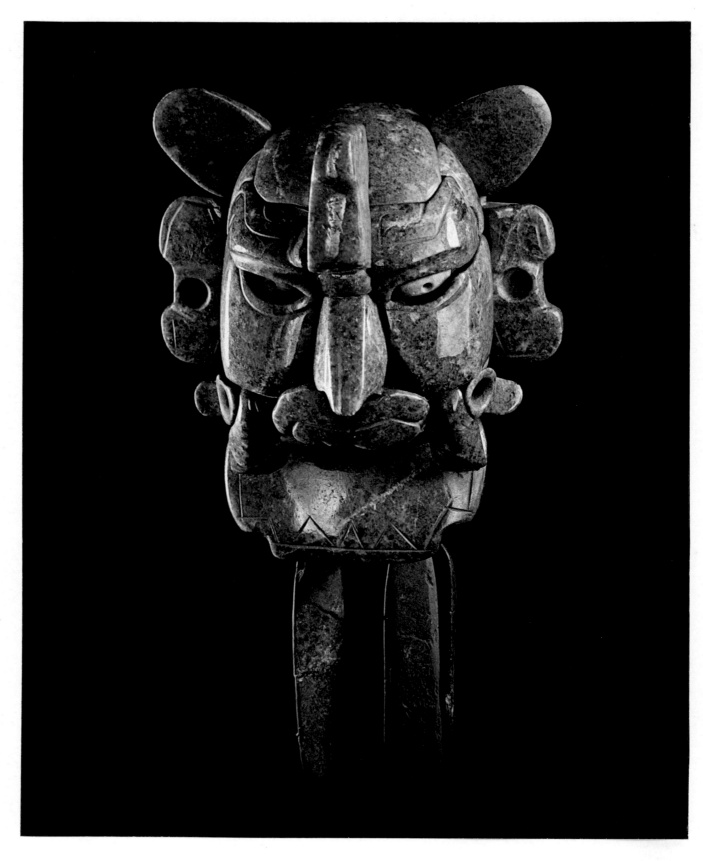

Bat mask, Monte Albán (Oaxaca): height, ca. 7 in. Zapotec culture, 3rd-8th century A.D. Zapotec culture was permeated by a sense of death. Lavish tombs and innumerable mortuary offerings were perhaps its most distinctive features. The bat, god of darkness and death, was prominent in the Zapotec mortuary cult. He is depicted in this striking mask of finely worked jadeite segments, with eyes of shell inlay, and pendants of differently colored slate.

ART AND ARCHAEOLOGY OF OAXACA

THE ZAPOTECS

The Zapotec culture flourished in the central valleys of the state of Oaxaca, especially at Etla, Tlacolula and Zimatlán. The origins of the Zapotecs are linked to the Olmec culture of the Gulf Coast and to Indian groups of southern Chiapas, the so-called "proto-Mayas". Perhaps for this reason the chronicles of the Zapotecs said they were descended from the jaguar, the favourite animal of the Olmecs, which was both a deity and a totem.

According to archaeological evidence, about 900 B.C. the Olmecs of the Gulf Coast began to spread throughout the isthmus of Tehuantepec. They occupied locations such as Juchitán, Laguna Zopre, Puerto Angel, Huamelulpán and Monte Albán. Thus began a period that has come to be called Monte Albán I (900-300 B.C.). During this epoch, pottery making was the dominant artistic form and more elaborate construction was initiated, as were a calendar, a system of numbers and hieroglyphics. The pottery of this period is characteristically monochromatic, in tones of black, white and gray. The most characteristic vessels, many of which have a simple spout, represent swimmers and animals. Web-footed plates, bottles and braziers with Olmec faces were other known forms, as well as miniature vases representing fish, frogs, snails and other animals.

Although earthwork mounds, platforms and various minor structures were constructed in other locations, the most important building site was at Monte Albán. There a tableland was created with artificial fill, retaining walls were raised, and the great base known as "Los Danzantes" was erected. It owes its name to the series of great component slabs, placed vertically and horizontally, and was decorated with figures of swimmers and other personages in dynamic attitudes (as if they were performing a dance), rendered in the artistic style of the Olmecs. The majority of these slabs contain hieroglyphics and numerals.

The next period, known as Monte Albán II (300-100 B.C.), is characterized by the introduction of certain pottery influences from the south. Among these are mammiform supports, labial and basal molding, fresco decoration, cameo technique, and tripod vessels. The last are frequently found throughout the Maya region as well, evidence that the Zapotecs had close contact with the Mayas. During this period mound J was built: it has a base indicating astronomical observations and is decorated with slabs. Tombs were built with display chambers and antechambers covered with vaulted roofs. Pottery offerings, especially clay urns with representations of deities, were placed within these tombs. Recognizable among these pottery offerings were the representations of the rain god Cocijo and the fire god Huehueteotl, as well as a deity with a bird mask and a bat god related to the death cult.

The following period, a transitional stage known as Monte Albán II-III (100 B.C.-200 A.D.), marked the beginning of the true Zapotec culture. Some Teotihuacán influence became noticeable in their ceramics, however, such as the flower-shaped vases and candelabra, double-spouted pots, censers and urns with representations of Tlaloc. This interval was followed by the zenith of Zapotec culture, during the periods called Monte Albán III A and III B after 200 A.D. The Zapotecs made impressive achievements in astronomy and devised a number system, a calendar, hieroglyphic writing and herbal medicine. They also excelled in minor arts such as pottery, goldsmith work and jewelry making. The ceremonial center of Monte Albán reached its maximum extension during this period. The plateau site was prepared for the construction of various structures, including ball courts, temple bases with double scapulary slabs, sunken patios with altars in the center, columned buildings and masonry chambers for the ruling class. The common people lived nearby in houses built of perishable materials.

The cult of the dead became more complex in this era, with rulers and priests being buried in elaborate tombs fitted out with staircases, antechambers and funerary vaults, having wall niches and sometimes mural decorations. Such tombs were built below the patios, or plazas, and also beneath the chambers and bases of the temples. Near the corpses were placed offerings consisting of personal objects, utensils, food-stuffs and huge clay urns with representations of the gods who protected the dead. These urns illustrated the polytheistic character of the Zapotec religion by the variety of divinities found portrayed on them.

The social and political organization of the Zapotecs was essentially theocratic, although it eventually acquired a certain militaristic cast. According to historical accounts, their principal officials were an all-powerful chief or cacique (*gocquitao*); a high priest (*huitjatoo*); secondary chiefs (*gocquis*); a series of judges (*quixiagas*) and sheriffs (*xiagas*), who attended to administrative and religious functions. The tradesmen (*benizanijas*) formed a special class as a result of the services they provided for the city. Markets and annual fairs were held in the various towns, and certain objects, such as copper tacks, were used as money. The Zapotecs obtained their food through agriculture, hunting, fishing and the gathering of wild edibles. They developed a terracing system for cultivating their land and, later, an artificial irrigation system of canals. At the time of the Spanish conquest they were using copper hoes for cultivation. The Zapotecs drew upon a great variety of raw materials for the manufacture of their implements, utensils, arms, ornaments and other personal articles. The Zapotec Indians deformed their skulls, mutilated their teeth and painted their bodies and faces as a means of beautifying and distinguishing themselves.

THE MIXTECS

The Zapotec culture gradually declined between 800 and 1200 A.D., mainly as a result of the incursions of the Mixtecs. This latter group came down from the surrounding mountains and gave rise to some centers such as Yagul, Mitla, Zaachila and Teotitlán. At the same time, new centers such as Teozacualco, Tilantengo, Coixtlahuaca and Yanhuitlán were established, where Mixtec culture flourished.

The Mixtecs preferred higher elevations, and in their territories they practiced agriculture, hunting, fishing and food gathering. With time they developed an advanced technology, especially in the mining of gold, silver and copper, from which they fashioned beautiful ornaments, arms and tools to work their lands. In metallurgy they acquired great mastery in the techniques of hammering, soldering, "lost wax" casting and filigree. With extraordinary imagination they made plated bracelets, pectoral disks with embossed designs, necklaces, rings and other ornamental accessories. They also carved admirably in onyx and alabaster, for elegantly-shaped vases; in rock-crystal, for necklace beads and lip plugs; in jade, for outline figurines of household gods; in wood, for masks covered with turquoise and shell mosaics or for drums and spears decorated in low relief. They also worked jaguar bone, carving calendar and religious motifs in low relief, with an artistry comparable to Chinese ivory miniatures.

The Mixtec artistic style displayed in their pottery, architectonic decoration and codices created a tradition which was fully assimilated by some groups and which influenced others to varying degrees. Their pottery was distinguished by glossy or dull-finished polychromatic decoration, usually with a repeated design of flowers, human tibia, skulls, hieroglyphs, gods or other motifs. The color range, as in the codices, tended to red, gray, yellow, black and orange. In architecture the Mixtecs followed the Zapotec mode of double scapulary slabs, but they enriched this basic form by decorating the façades

Urn, from Monte Albán (Oaxaca): height, ca. 26 ½ in. Zapotec culture, Classic period, 3rd-7th century A.D. Mosaic wall (reproduction), from Mitla (Oaxaca). Mixtec culture, post-Classic period, 13th-15th century A.D. After perhaps a thousand years of existence, the Zapotec culture was overcome by the Mixtecs. Here, the qualities of the two cultures are reflected in a masterful Zapotec urn set before the technically superb carved stone mosaic from Mitla, the great Mixtec ceremonial center.

of their buildings.   Hundreds of tiny stones were assembled, stuccoed and painted to form bands of repeated designs.   They also constructed elaborate cruciform stone tombs for their rulers, with niches and façades decorated with stone mosaics.   The beauty of Mixtec architecture can be seen at such archaeological sites as Mitla, Zaachila, Teotitlán, Coixtlahuaca and Xaaga.

Mixtec codices were made on long, folded strips of paper or animal skins. They form an exceptional pictorial tradition and are a source of information that is only now beginning to be studied. Codices such as the Selden, Nuttall, Bodley, Vindobonensi and Columbino, present with great colorfulness, knowledge and imagination such subjects as Mixtec genealogies, historical events, calendar and religious motifs and battles and conquests.   In sum, the Mixtecs were great painters of codices, potters and goldsmiths; skilled craftsmen, whose work exhibited high technical standards and a refined sense of style. The Zapotecs may be described as more intellectually accomplished and better architects than other Indian groups.   They also imbued their work with a greater religious awareness.

Tripod vessel with human skeleton, from Zaachila (Oaxaca): height, ca. 12 in. Mixtec culture, post-Classic period, 11th-15th century A.D. The familiar presence of death is found even in the utensils of everyday life.

Below :

Whistling jug with warrior, from the Valley of Oaxaca: height, ca. 6¾ in. Mixtec culture, Classic period, 6th-8th century A.D. A Mixtec warrior bearing a shield hurls a projectile with his dart thrower *(atl-atl)*, a primitive weapon common to the early people of Mesoamerica. The jug is musical, for it whistles when tipped if water is placed inside.

Clay head representing life and death, from Soyaltepec (Oaxaca): height, ca. 11¾ in. Zapotec culture, Classic period, 3rd-7th century A.D. "Danzantes" (reproduction), from Monte Albán (Oaxaca). Zapotec culture, pre-Classic period, 6th-2nd century B.C. Dynamic Olmec figures carved in relief on retaining walls show the influence of the Gulf Coast on Monte Albán I. The figures may represent the sick and deformed. Life and death unite in the remarkable Zapotec clay head.

Jaguar urns, from Monte Albán (Oaxaca): height, ca. 14½ and 16¾ in. Zapotec culture, Classic period, 3rd-8th century A.D.   The Zapotec funerary urns, beginning as simple unadorned pots, soon became in the classic period true commemorative sculptures.   The jaguar as a funeral offering indicated aristocratic or priestly rank.   The Museum gardens are the background for these two striking zoomorphic urns.

Large polychrome jaguar urn from Monte Albán (Oaxaca): height, ca. 33 in. Zapotec culture, Classic period, 3rd-8th century A.D. The jaguar was feared and worshipped by most of the pre-Columbian peoples, from the Mayas to the Zapotecs. His menacing, feline grace characterizes this monumental polychrome urn, which held funerary fire, and received or conveyed water and other gifts to the gods.

Funerary urn with face, from Monte Albán (Oaxaca): height, ca. 31 in. Zapotec culture, early Classic period, 1st-3rd century A.D. A typical Zapotec face is preserved in this monumental clay urn. In the background is a photomural of Monte Albán, the city built for the gods. For the construction of this huge ceremonial center, a mountain top was leveled to form a gigantic terrace or platform, on which temples and pyramids were erected.

Urn in the form of an old man, from Monte Albán (Oaxaca): height, ca. 18 in. Zapotec culture, Classic period, 3rd-8th century A.D. A profusion of funerary edifices and urns to be placed within them is typical of the Classic Zapotec period. The ancient Zapotecs are represented here in the figure of an old man, bent under the weight of his cape, jewelry and elaborate headdress of fine feathers.

Urn in the form of a woman, from Monte Albán (Oaxaca): height, ca. 13¾ in. Zapotec culture, Classic period, 3rd-8th century A.D. The contemporary Zapotec woman of the Oaxaca area still dresses much like this woman of some twelve centuries ago, with *quechquemitl*, *huipil*, sandals, earplugs, and beautiful necklaces. Although she continues to braid her long black hair with colored cotton cords, she no longer files her teeth for purposes of beauty.

Funerary urns, from the state of Oaxaca: Zapotec culture, Classic period, 3rd-9th century A.D. These funerary urns are a rich testimony of the respect the dead enjoyed in classic Zapotec culture. The pride, the wealth and love of beauty of this ancient culture are expressed in these strong and graceful figural urns that were made to accompany the dead to the abode of the gods. The human face, rendered with skill and refinement, is made nearly into a portrait. The persons shown in these sculptures

are dressed in garments denoting high rank. Their hands are often held across their breast in a gesture of defense, or extended along their sides and knees in a gesture of calm. The elaborate majesty and beauty of the headdresses is a remarkable affirmation of life after death. Cosejo, the Zapotec rain god, was often depicted this way, elegantly crowned with a ritual headgear of symbolic snake heads or feathers. Technical perfection, extraordinary and beautiful decoration mark these images.

Jewelry, from Monte Albán (Oaxaca): Mixtec culture, 13th-15th century A.D. As Teotihuacán was the cultural center of the highland, so Monte Albán or "White Mountain," as the Spaniards called it, was the seat of the cultures of Oaxaca, a military and commercial key to southwestern Mexico. It was a city of many buildings, temples, palaces and possibly an astronomical observatory. One of the greatest finds in the area was tomb no. 7. Originally it was a burial vault built by the Zapotecs. Centuries later it was used by the Mixtecs for the burial of dignitaries, who were interred with what is perhaps the most outstanding pre-Hispanic treasure ever found. The Mixtecs were great masters of the techniques of working with rock-crystal, jade and bone and of shaping gold, silver, and copper into imaginative jewelry such as bracelets, necklaces, pectorals, earplugs, rings, tiny bells and other luxury articles. Outstanding in this group, as exhibited in the museum, are on the left the mask of Xipe Totec and, on the right, the great pectoral with an image of Mictlantecuhtli, god of the Underworld.

Colossal stone head, from La Venta (Tabasco): height, ca. 7ft. 3 in. Olmec culture, 12th-6th century B.C. The image of man becomes mountain-like: the giant Negroid head, endowed with the fierce traits of the jaguar, his enemy and his god, seems to emerge directly from the soil and defy the jungle. Found in the tropical forests of southern Veracruz and Tabasco, these sculptural masterpieces are testaments of the enigmatic and remarkably advanced Olmec culture.

THE GULF COAST CULTURES

Gliding over the water in barks they came
In many groups
And alighted there at water's edge
Along the northern shore
And where they left their vessels,
Panutla lies.

SAHAGUN.

THE OLMECS

Olmec culture has been the subject of dedicated investigation by Mexican archaeologists for many years. Several theories have been advanced to explain its origin, but adequate information is still lacking.

The name Olmec derives from a Nahuatl word for rubber, a product which—according to the earliest Spanish chronicles—was the major source of this society's wealth. Already by the time of the Spanish Conquest, the Olmecs were known to have been the oldest civilized inhabitants of Mexico, and as such, other Indian cultures recognized them as their prime source.

The Olmecs played an extremely important role in the formation and development of the early phase of the principal Mesoamerican cultures. Not only did they have the most advanced of the pre-Classic Mesoamerican cultures, both technically and artistically, but they also greatly influenced various other cultures spread over a vast territory. For example, Olmec features may be recognized in the pre-Classic of the Maya zone in Uaxactun; in the formative phases of the Zapotec (Monte Albán I) and Mixtec (Montenegro) cultures of Oaxaca; in many pre-Classic sites of central Mexico such as Tlatilco, Las Bocas, Chalcatzingo, Gualupita and Tlapacoya as well as in numerous (as yet unexcavated) ancient sites in the state of Guerrero. For these reasons, the Olmec culture is often considered a "mother culture" whose elements make up a common substratum of great importance in the formation of the first pre-Classic Mesoamerican village cultures. The most important centers inhabited by the Olmec people were located in the jungles of southern Veracruz and Tabasco, principally in the mountains of Los Tuxtlas and in the Toralá and Coatzacoalcos river basins. La Venta in Tabasco and San Lorenzo Tenochtitlán and Tres Zapotes in Veracruz possess the richest manifestations of this culture.

The origins of the Olmec culture may be traced back as far as 1500 B.C. Its phase of greatest splendor occurred from the ninth to the third century B.C.; subsequently it declined, until it merged with other cultures at the beginning of the Classic period, about the third century A.D.

The characteristic art objects found at the Olmec sites are vigorous and simple in form; the styles may be strange, but they are also unmistakeable. Stone was unquestionably the medium in which the Olmec artist gave fullest reign to his creative genius. The materials he most commonly used were basalt for large sculptures, and many other kinds of stone—ranging from jade to quartzites and soapstone—for smaller sculptures. The stones' own shadings were generally used with great skill. The majority of these sculptures are of human beings with notably constant characteristics such as broad faces, mongoloid eyes, heavy eyelids and protruding eyeballs, flat noses and broad nostrils of Negroid type. One striking characteristic of Olmec sculpture is the formation of the mouth, which is open and often shows the gums. The upper lip is broad, flat and raised as if grimacing; the corners of the mouth are strongly curved downwards, so that the lower lip is also strongly curved. This is the shape of what has been called the "Olmec mouth." It has been sometimes suggested that this feline gesture makes a symbolic reference to the mouth of the jaguar, an animal which roamed the jungles of the Olmec area and appears to have been worthy of Olmec worship.

Many different kinds of monoliths were carved from stone blocks, some weighing up to twenty-five tons. These must have been transported scores of miles through jungles, swamps and rivers, since basalt is not readily available in the Olmec area. The best known of these monoliths are the giant Olmec heads. Some of these are eight to nine feet high and weigh up to ten tons. Four were found at La Venta, and others were carved at San Lorenzo and Tres Zapotes. The nearest quarries to La Venta are, for example, eighty miles away and transportation of the heavy stones must have been by water. Besides Olmec heads, the large sculpture repertory includes huge altars decorated with statues in high and low relief, monolithic sarcophagi, and rectangular slabs of tables supported by atlantes. Stelae, or funerary pillars, bearing representations of dignitaries and ceremonies, are accompanied by glyphs and numerals, which are evidence of the existence of one of the oldest calendar and writing systems in Mesoamerica. All this monumental sculpture, like much else related to this enigmatic civilization, remains surprising and curious, but an astonishing plastic force and imagination give these works great individuality.

This plastic power and individuality was also poured into the making of delicate jadeite jewels, ornaments and other human and animal representations. Among these were anthropomorphic jaguar figures which were frequently placed as funerary offerings. These figures, unlike Olmec heads or sarcophagi, have been found in non-Olmec sites and provide one of the most direct and explicit evidences of the wide-reaching influence of the Olmecs in Mesoamerican civilizations. In addition to figures representing a jaguar deity, the Olmecs carved "axes" from several stones, quite often from a blue-green jade which is rarely seen except in Olmec artefacts. A large group of these was found in La Venta, containing six incised "axes" and fifteen upright human figures. Other "axes" conform to the "baby face" Olmec type with broad nostrils and monstrous mouth, but with a definitely human shape to the head, shoulders and arms.

The best examples of Olmec ceramics have not been found in their ceremonial centers of the Gulf Coast, but have appeared most frequently at pre-Classic sites in central Mexico, where Olmec influence was most strongly implanted. The fusion of Olmec artistic ideas and styles with the skillful, long established ceramic techniques of the village peoples of the central valleys, gave rise to some very refined examples of this art. Their figural sculpture in clay or stone is almost exclusively of infantile beings with expressions of suffering or cruelty. Also very common are representations of dwarfs and persons with various congenital defects.

The known Olmec architectural constructions are not very impressive and are limited to platforms and mounds made of earth and undressed masonry of varying size and shape. Perhaps the outstanding example of their architecture is to be found at a site in La Venta, where there is a great main mound, with other smaller ones distributed along a long central axis. The layout is interesting, since it demonstrates certain principles of town planning and may have been an important influence in the planning of later great cities such as Teotihuacán, which was also oriented along a central axis or avenue. Among other significant features of Olmec architecture are the tombs built with huge monolithic columns, and the rectangular green stone tiles forming mosaics that represent typically Olmec-style jaguar heads.

Clearly, much scientific research remains to be done in order to learn, with greater certainty, the role of the Olmecs in the birth and development of the high Mesoamerican civilizations. The wide diffusion of Olmec styles, their great antiquity and the strong individualism of their artistic creations, continue to make the Olmec problem one of the most intriguing in Mexican archaeology. The remote cultural interaction between these coastal and jungle peoples protected by the jaguar, and the creators of the central highlands' cultures, whose symbolic animal may have been the eagle, constitutes one of the important themes in Mexican archaeology—further study of which might very well explain the surprising technical and cultural advances achieved in pre-Columbian Mexico.

Quetzalcóatl stele, from Castillo de Teayo (Veracruz): height, ca. 11 ft. Huastec culture, post-Classic period, 11th-14th century A.D. ▶ The god Quetzalcóatl, wearing a conical cap and snailshell pectoral, stands in the form of a stele. The Olmec "athlete" sits in the background, and through a window a gigantic Olmec head is visible. The basalt stone, used here, is typical of Olmec large sculpture.

Jadeite plaque with carved jaguar god, from region of La Mixteca (Oaxaca): height, ca. 8½ in. Olmec culture, 12th-6th century B.C. The incredible creative force evident in the huge stone works of the Olmecs is equally impressive in this delicate plaque which once again shows the ferocious aspect of the jaguar.

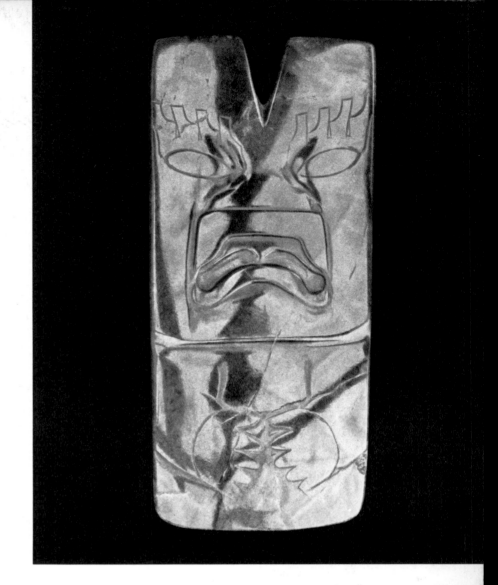

◄ Carved jadeite head, from Tenango (State of Mexico). The Olmec culture, artistically and technically the most advanced of pre-Classic Mesoamerica, strongly influenced a vast territory. This group created strange and magnificent works of art such as this enigmatic countenance with its characteristic elongated skull, mongoloid eyes and feline expression. The mouth shape is so representative that it is often referred to as the "Olmec mouth."

Jadeite figure, from El Tejar (Veracruz): height, 5¾ in. Olmec culture, 12th-6th century B.C. This exquisitely carved figurine of an Olmec seated in Oriental fashion attests a possible connection with the East for this jungle culture. The Olmec is considered a "mother culture," since its basic elements appear throughout Mesoamerica.

A ritual cache with sixteen figurines carved from jadeite and serpentine, from la Venta (Veracruz): height ca. 8 in. Olmec culture, 4th century B.C.-3rd century A.D. This extraordinary grouping was mounted in the museum exactly as it was found in the archaeological excavations made at the important ceremonial center of La Venta, Tabasco. Several jadeite "hatchets" are grouped together with sixteen figurines in a circle, indicating perhaps the celebration of some ritual or ceremony. Because one of the figurines, in reddish stone, is noticeably inferior artistically, it has been suggested that the scene represents the impending execution of a prisoner or sacrificial victim. Although much research has been devoted to the chronology, area of development and influence of Olmec culture, a good many of the particular works through which we know it are still to be more accurately understood and explained.

Hollow clay figure wearing a jaguar skin, from Atlihuayán (Morelos): height, ca. 12½ in. Olmec culture 11th-9th century B.C. Man and jaguar again become one in this sculpture of an important personage or a witch doctor. He wears a jaguar skin that covers his head, shoulders and back.

Athlete or ball player, from Minatitlán (Veracruz): height, ca. 25¾ in. ▶ Olmec culture, 12th-6th century B.C. The "Olmec athlete," also known as the "wrestler," is a masterpiece of pre-Hispanic sculpture, which captures with extraordinary austerity the inherent force, movement and life of the human figure. Probably a depiction of a player in the ritual ball game, it is the finest realistic portrait we have of Olmec man.

Jadeite plaque with engraved Olmec face, from La Venta (Tabasco): height, ca. 7 in. Olmec culture, 12th-6th century B.C. The angry, contorted expression of the face on this plaque was created by a culture very much aware of cruelty. The smaller Olmec designs, incised over the main motif, are a common characteristic of Olmec lapidary art.

CENTRAL VERACRUZ

Central Veracruz is the name loosely applied to a culture area, in the central zone of the Gulf of Mexico coast, which is bounded on the north by the Cazones River and which borders on Olmec territory at the Tuxtla mountains to the south. During pre-Hispanic times, it was densely populated and constituted a veritable mosaic of differing cultures. Many gaps exist in our knowledge about these groups and their interrelations, but nonetheless, this is an incredibly rich archaeological zone.

The Remojadas culture, beginning in the eighth century B.C., is the most fully and accurately described pre-Classic style in Central Veracruz. The outstanding quality of its ceramics, the infinite variety of vessels and the extraordinary human figurines, were worthy predecessors of the remarkable flowering of this art in Central Veracruz. Other pre-Classic sites such as El Trapiche and Viejon show Olmec influence.

El Tajín in Central Veracruz, named after the great ceremonial center near the town of Papantla, is the best-known site for the culture of the Classic period in this area. The complex erected by the Tajín people included great palaces, colonnades, plazas, ball courts and stepped substructures for their temples. The buildings were decorated with relief slabs and fretwork friezes made of hewn stone set with mosaic.

The famous Temple of the Niches in El Tajín is perhaps the most graceful and elegant of the pyramidal structures of ancient Mexico. The ruins of Yohualichán on the Puebla border constitute another important site, vestiges of a culture that reached its zenith between the sixth and tenth centuries A.D.

A high level of technical finish and artistic quality was achieved in the famous "yokes," "axes," "palmate stones" and "padlocks". These beautiful and enigmatic objects, exquisitely carved in stone, seem to have some relation to the ritual of the ball game. In fact, in many stelae with sculptural bas-reliefs belonging to the Classical period of Central Veracruz, as well as in some clay figurines of the same culture, one may clearly notice objects which maintain an absolute identity with the "palmate" stones and the "yokes," forming a rather permanent part of the equipment and appearance of personages related to the ritual ball game, which undoubtedly had a relation with the practice of human sacrifice. Sculptural reliefs on the slab stones of the building of the Ball Game, at El Tajín, are especially illustrative in this respect. Logically, the stone sculpture of these objects must be interpreted as ceremonial representations of their originals, which in order to be employed during the ball game, must have been made of light materials.

Central Veracruz ceramics are distinguished by large, hollow clay figures that are outstanding for their realism and expressiveness. Also characteristic is the "smiling head" type, which clearly expresses an animated, festive attitude that is rare in pre-Columbian art and which seems to have been peculiar to the creators of this culture. Among other details heightening this mood is the constant repetition of spirals, meanders, fretwork and other serpentine decorative elements with a marked rhythm and movement. Whether in architecture, stone relief, sculpture or pottery, the art of the El Tajín culture seems to have the warm and sensual quality of the coastal region in which it flowered.

The Central Veracruz area was occupied during the post-Classic period and until the Conquest by descendants of the earlier inhabitants, whose culture was influenced by the Toltecs and later by the Aztecs of Central Mexico. An important site of this period is the Isla de Sacrificios, where remarkable alabaster vessels were found, along with plumbate ware, with its bright metallic reflections characteristic of the Toltec epoch. The cities of Quiahuiztlán and Cempoala, whose architecture was obviously derived from the Aztecs, also belong to this epoch. However, from pre-Classic times, the brilliant ceramic tradition of Central Veracruz continued to bear influence until a late date and resulted in, for example, representations of Aztec gods that took on great plastic qualities in the hands of the native coastal sculptors.

Hollow clay serpent head, from Acatlán de Pérez Figueroa (Oaxaca): height, ca. 30 in. Veracruz culture, 14th-16th century A.D. This sacred serpent, molded with a sensual realism in rhythmic and elegant lines, expresses artistically the warm human qualities of the central Veracruz coastal region. With clear Aztec influences, it probably depicts Xiuhcóatl, the fire serpent. The pottery head served as a brazier; burning coals were dropped into the top, and smoke came out through the jaws.

"Yoke" with representation of an owl, from state of Veracruz: height, ca. 5¼ in. Central Veracruz culture, Classic period, 7th-10th century A.D. Three main types of sculpture, the "yokes," "axes" and "palmate stones," are so named since their symbolism has not yet been wholly understood. Different scholars have offered different accounts of their functions; they may have been associated with a ritual ball game. Sculptural and technical perfection characterizes this closed yoke decorated with the figure of an owl in delicate relief. The yokes, actually used in the ball game, were made of leather and protected the player's hips, with which the ball was struck.

Huehueteotl, the old god of fire, from Cerro de las Olesas (Veracruz): height, ca. 34½ in. Veracruz culture, 5th-8th century A.D. This monumental hollow clay figure of Huehueteotl, one of the most characteristic religious effigies of this period, is bent with age. On his head he bears the huge sacred brazier, which holds the primordial fire from which all life originates.

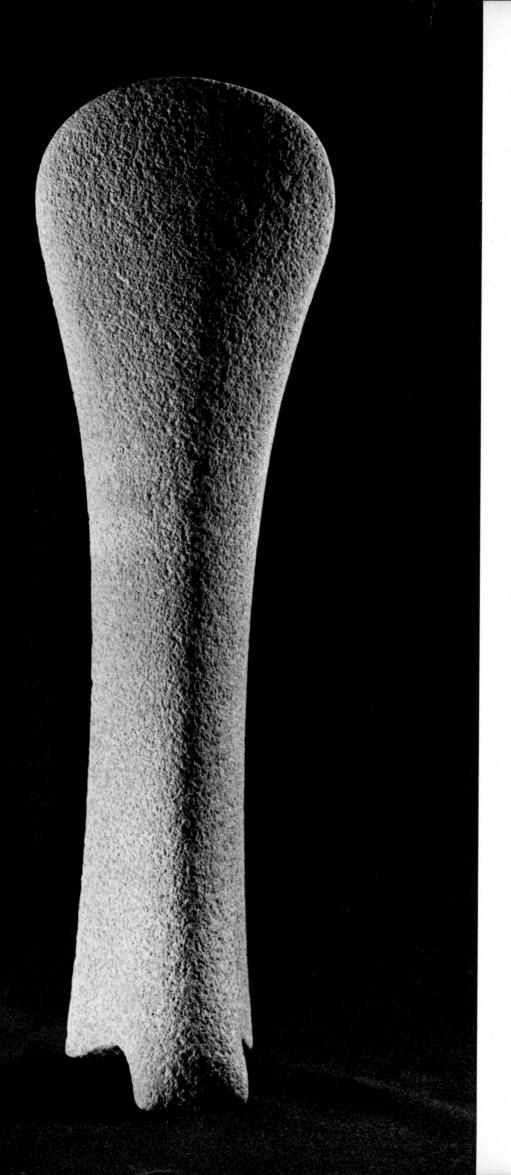

Smooth palmate stone, from state of Veracruz: height, ca. 30 in. Central Veracruz culture, Classic period, 7th-10th century A.D. This undecorated palmate stone evidences a notable purity and elegance of line.

Right:

Palmate stone with hands in prayerful gesture, from state of Veracruz: height, ca. 16 in. Central Veracruz culture, Classic period, 7th-10th century A.D. These stylized hands in an attitude of supplication, furnish a striking example of the resemblance of ancient Veracruz sculpture to that of certain modern artists.

Overleaf:

Several hollow clay "smiling head" figurines, from state of Veracruz: height, ca. 7 to 10½ in. Central Veracruz culture, Classic period, 7th-10th century A.D. In contrast to the fierce expression of the other Olmec faces, here a chorus of childish laughter rings out and the open arms gesture with joy. These examples of typical smiling figurines are of different styles and from different localities, but all demonstrate one of the distinctive features of the culture of central Veracruz, as well as one of the few expressions of joyous emotion in pre-Columbian art.

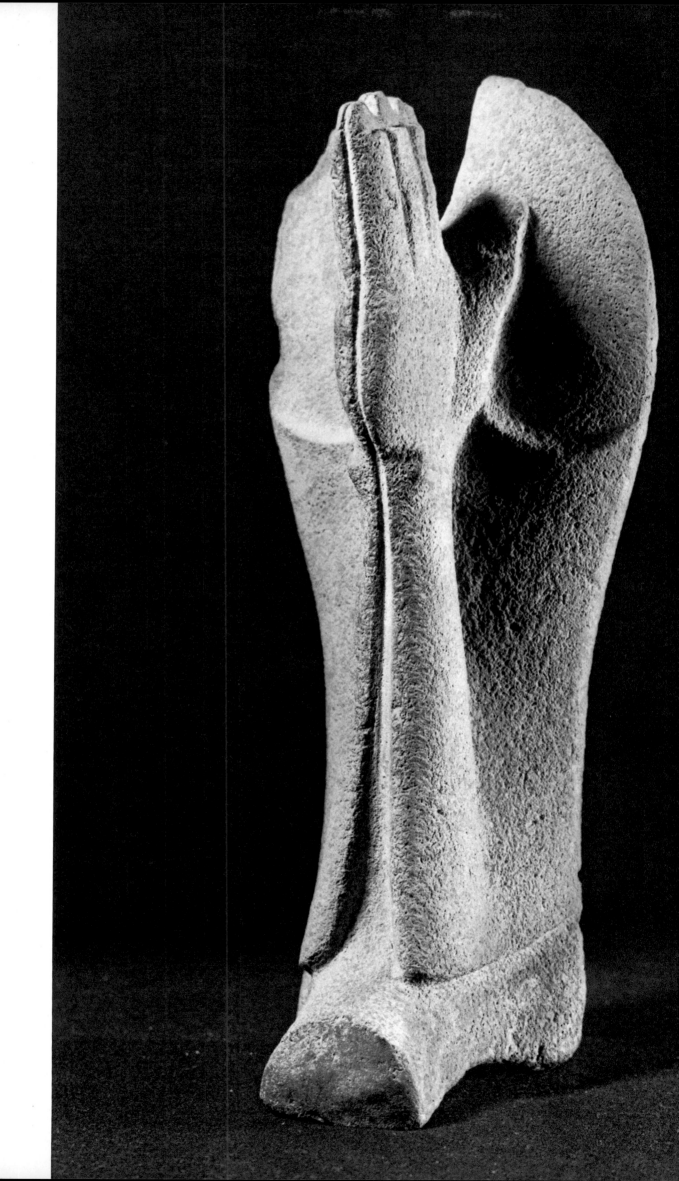

THE HUASTECS

The pre-Hispanic Huastecs inhabited northern Veracruz and neighboring regions of the states of Tamaulipas, San Luis Potosí and Hidalgo. The close relationship of the Huastec and Maya languages seems to indicate that these two peoples shared a common culture in remote times. Subsequently, the Huastecs became isolated in the north by the infiltration of other groups which, acting as a wedge, established themselves throughout the central and southern Veracruz area and in Tabasco.

The geographical location of Huastec culture in the outermost northeastern region of pre-Hispanic Mesoamerica gives this area a rather special interest in the study of the ancient relations among the cultures of central Mexico and the cultures that at the same time flourished in the southeast of the United States. In fact, the Huastec area seems to have been a kind of corridor for the influences that spread northward since the oldest of times. Many Mesoamerican traits found in the archaeology of the southern United States came to this area by way of Huastec territory.

The Huastec culture developed over a long period, stretching from its pre-Classic phase in the seventeenth century B.C. to the Spanish Conquest. Pottery excavated near Pánuco (Veracruz) has helped to establish the sequence of this prolonged evolution. During the earliest stages, the Huastecs had village cultures possessing all the general characteristics of the pre-Classic period. Numerous fired-clay figurines, similar to those still produced in central Mexico, were found (principally in the deepest strata) at Pánuco and El Ebano, in San Luis Potosí. Like many other pre-Columbian peoples, the Huastecs reached an artistic and cultural peak in the Classic period, which extended from the fourth to the ninth century A.D. Their densely populated territory included small ceremonial and dwelling centers made up of groups of mounds varying in size and form. Huastec architecture, though of great variety, was technically poor in both layout and form. Their architecture was characterized by rounded corners and circular or semi-circular buildings generally associated with the cult of their most important deity, Ehecatl-Quetzalcóatl, the wind god. Their temples were constructed on large platforms with many substructures.

The Huastecs were, however, outstanding sculptors in stone. Their many figures of gods and dignitaries were, for the most part, highly stylized, but they also produced such marvelous naturalistic pieces as the world-famous "Adolescent" of Tamuín. Strange figures of humpbacked old men supporting themselves on staffs are also fairly common, and these may be representations of Huehueteotl, the old god. Another dramatically expressed theme in various Huastec sculpture is the life-death duality, which was frequently worked into the same piece.

Shell work is outstanding among the Huastecs' minor arts. Perhaps no other pre-Hispanic people employed this material so skillfully or imaginatively. The infinite variety of ornaments they produced in great quantities include necklaces, bracelets, rings, ear and noseplugs, jointed human figurines and splendid gorgets with delicately-carved mythological scenes. Their pottery has a highly individual style. Predominant are vessels based on vegetal forms with stirrup handles or stirrup spouts. The anthropomorphic jugs are equally outstanding. The clay is almost white, contrasting sharply with the dark decoration. Solid clay figurines with bulbous legs and narrow waists are other distinctive forms.

Like many of the other regions of Mesoamerica, Huastec territory was subjugated by the Aztecs from central Mexico in the centuries immediately before the Spanish Conquest, so that there developed a mixture of religious ideas and artistic styles. The site of Castillo de Teayo (Veracruz), with its Aztec pyramid and many extraordinary sculptures, is particularly representative of the material culture of the Huastecs of this late phase.

The "Adolescent" of Tamuín, from Tamuín (San Luis Potosí): height, ca. 3 ft. 9 in. Huastec culture, Classic period, 7th-10th century A.D. ▶
This statue is one of the masterpieces of Huastec culture. The beautifully proportioned body is decorated with delicately incised symbolic and mythological reliefs. It is thought to represent the young god Quetzalcóatl. On his back he carries the sun as an indication of the newborn day. Huastec statues are almost always anthropomorphic, have rigorously geometric stylized forms and are powerfully simple.

Xilonen (or Centeocihuatl), "Goddess of the Young Corn," from state of Veracruz: height, ca. 32 ½ in. Huastec culture, 12th-15th ►
century A.D. The Huastecs, who generally inhabited northern Veracruz, were outstanding stone sculptors. They absorbed the themes
and stylistic features of Teotihuacán, as well as those of the Olmec and Mayan civilizations. The goddess, kneeling in an attitude
common to the women of ancient Mesoamerica, wears a headdress composed of ears of corn.

Cream-colored vessel in the form of a seated monkey, from state of Veracruz: height, ca. 7 ¼ in. Huastec culture, 12th-15th
century A.D. The monkey *(ozomatli)*, a frequently-depicted animal in pre-Columbian representations, was related symbolically
to feasting and fertility. It is generally carved in obsidian or alabaster, and is seen in various shapes and poses. This remarkable representation wears a necklace, and its tail serves as a spout. It looks ahead with an astonished expression.

Burial crypt of the Temple of the Inscriptions (replica). *(Foreground)* Jadeite mosaic mask and necklace, from Palenque (Chiapas): height of mask, ca. 8¾ in. Maya culture, 6th-7th century A.D. The Mayas, perhaps the most intellectually, artistically and technically advanced of the Mesoamerican groups, developed their culture for more than twenty-five centuries in southern Mexico and northern central America. This crypt is one of the latest and most dramatic archaeological discoveries relating to this civilization. Here we see the great monolithic sarcophagus containing the skeleton of a high dignitary. The jadeite mosaic mask and necklace were part of the mortuary offerings.

MAYAN ART AND ARCHAEOLOGY

> We are only guardians of things, oh friends,
> During our sojourn on earth;
> Tomorrow or the next day,
> As the heart desires, oh giver of life,
> We shall go, friends, to his abode.
>
> POPOL VUH.

Of all the pre-Columbian cultures, the Mayas' extraordinary intellectual, artistic and technical advances present a summit of development and refinement. This civilization has received perhaps greater attention from archaeologists, ethnologists, linguists and historians than any other area of Indian America. The Maya zone covers a vast part of southern Mesoamerica. In Mexico it encompasses all of Chiapas, Quintana Roo, Yucatán, Campeche and most of Tabasco, and it also extends into Guatemala and British Honduras. The types of environment range from the tropical rain forest of Chiapas and Guatemalan Petén to the evergreen-covered mountains and plateaus of the Yucatán Peninsula.

The beginnings of the Maya culture have been placed in the eleventh or twelfth centuries B.C. Definition of the most ancient pre-Classic, or formative, period is based largely on studies of the pottery of the highlands and of Guatemalan Petén, with the regions of Kaminaljuyú and Uaxactun having contributed most to the knowledge of these early epochs. Interesting examples of architecture exhibiting certain Olmec features appear in Uaxactun Petén, for the Mayas were heirs to the Olmecs.

In the Classic period, Maya culture reached its zenith. Many important ceremonial centers constructed during this era were located predominantly in the southern part of the Maya territory. The best known are Copán in Honduras; Tikal, Quirigua and Piedras Negras in Guatemala; Yaxchilán, Bonampak and Palenque in Chiapas and Coba in southern Yucatán. During the Late Classic period, new architectural styles flourished over a broad area of the Yucatán Peninsula. These modes are known as Puuc Chenes and Rio Bec and are associated with such important ruins as Uxmal, Kabah, Labna, Sayil, Chacmultun, Hochob and Xpuhil, all of which are in Mexican territory.

During the post-Classic period, starting in the ninth and tenth centuries A.D., a relationship with central Mexico can be discerned in certain decorative motifs, sculpture and architecture. This so-called "Maya-Toltec phase" is principally characteristic of such sites as Chichén-Itzá in Yucatán and Tulum on the Caribbean coast of Quintana Roo. After this time, however, Maya culture gradually declined until the Spanish Conquest. But even so, Maya civilization lasted two thousand seven hundred years.

The social and spiritual aspects of the Maya civilization in its Classic period of splendor are known, though imperfectly, through interpretation of numerous archaeological vestiges. Sculptured reliefs, mural or pottery paintings, clay figurines, funerary practices, civil and religious architecture and, finally, some rare original codices or pictorial manuscripts preserved from the pre-Hispanic period have provided much information about the Mayas. Aspects of their daily life have become known from the chronicles, written immediately after the conquest of Yucatán by various Spanish historians and priests. Bishop Diego de Landa, a Franciscan missionary, collected in 1556 an invaluable fund of information concerning the traditions of the Mayas during the last centuries of their independent life.

As among other pre-Hispanic peoples of Mesoamerica, all aspects of Mayan art and daily life were governed by a fundamental religious orientation. The principal Mayan deities are known mainly through their pictorial representations in the Dresden codex, one of three Mayan texts dating from before the Conquest, and are distinguished by their diverse facial and corporeal characteristics and peculiar dress.

For a people whose survival was so dependent upon abundant harvests, it is not surprising that their most important gods were those connected with water, rain, fertility and maize. Chac, the god of rain, equivalent to Tlaloc in central Mexico, is perhaps the god who appears with the greatest frequency in Mayan art. He is characterized by his large, pendulous nose—probably a stylized representation of the serpent, which was closely related to rain in the mythologies of many ancient peoples of the New World.

Other important gods of the Mayan pantheon, conventionally identified with alphabetical letters by some researchers, include: the god "K," who, like the god Chac, is related to the wind that impels the rain-bearing clouds; the god "D" is Itzamna, lord of the heavens and son of Hunab-Ku, the principal creator of life, who is characterized as a wrinkled old man with a single tooth; Kinich-Ahau is the sun god, or god "G," almost always represented with enormous squared eyes and filed teeth; the god of maize, god "E," is represented as a young man with pleasant features who often bears on his head the stylized symbol of a young maize plant; and Ah-Puch, god "A," who presided over death and the nether world, is generally shown either as a skeleton or with a black-spotted body, undoubtedly indicative of decaying flesh. Other Mayan deities associated with death are the god "F," linked with human sacrifice and corresponding to Xipe Totec of the religion of central Mexico, and Ixtab, the goddess of sacrifice, characterized by a rope hung around her neck. It was believed that sacrificial suicide assured entrance into heaven. In the centuries immediately before the Spanish Conquest, the god Kukulcán, the plumed serpent, became predominant in the Maya-Toltec culture of Yucatán, as a local equivalent to Quetzalcóatl of central Mexico. He had led, legend said, a tribe of Toltecs called the Itzá, who renamed a Mayan center Chichén Itzá, and eventually combined with the Maya to create a final and distinct phase of civilization in the area.

The Mayan religion was characterized essentially by fixed groups of deities, generally conceived in groups of four, that were synthetized into a single god. This concept was directly related to the four cardinal compass points and the symbolic colors representative of each: that is, red for the east, white for the north, black for the west and yellow for the south. Duality also prevailed in the Mayan religion; many of the gods were associated with both good and evil, heaven and the underworld, life and death, the masculine and feminine gender and both animal and human form.

Valuable information concerning the political and social organization of the pre-Columbian Maya, during the Late Classic period, can be deduced from the famous mural paintings of Bonampak and from the information collected by Bishop Landa. The *halachuinic*, or warrior chief, seems to have been the principal military and political leader of the Maya provinces. This hereditary position involved acting as judge, high priest, and supreme military commander. Lower in the hierarchy were *batabs*, or regents, of individual towns, who headed the local council and performed internal duties of a judicial, military and administrative nature. The *batabs* were appointed to their posts by the *halachuinics* of the corresponding province and in wartime were assisted by commanders, or *nacoms*, who organized the army with the aid of warrior captains called *holcans*, who were paid for their professional services.

The Maya populace was, however, predominantly composed of commoners, whose position in the social hierarchy depended upon personal wealth and the proximity of their dwellings to the ceremonial centers. The status of servant and slave existed, and those who had committed crimes or who were captured in wars were taken into servitude. This condition was not hereditary, and freedom could be purchased. No other pre-Columbian civilization has left so many or such well preserved architectural monuments

This section of the Maya Room was assigned a double height in order to permit dignified and spacious presentation of large examples of ▶ Mayan sculpture. Prominent among these are carved stone stelae and lintels, which the Mayas erected at certain fixed periods of time and inscribed with extensive hieroglyphic texts and dates. Only the most recent of these have been deciphered. Stelae with a great variety of ceremonial scenes in relief, with descriptive hieroglyphic writing, were also erected in commemoration of important events in Mayan life. The large windows permit penetration into the room of the temples of Hochob and Bonampak, which were reconstructed in the garden.

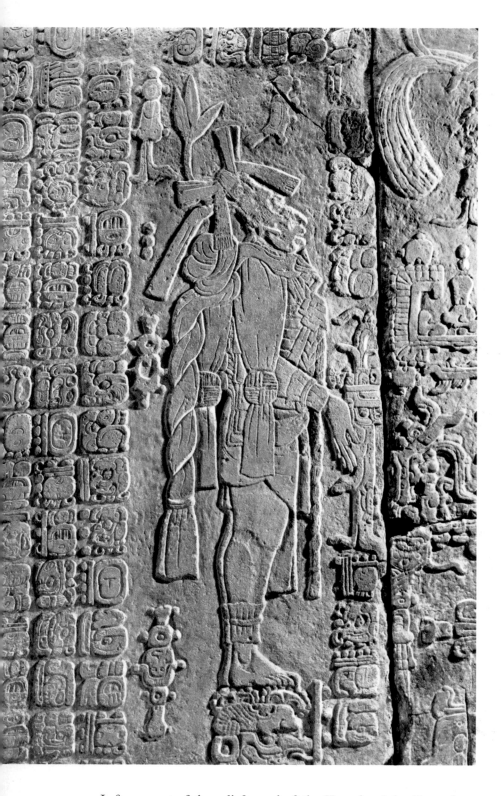

Left segment of the relief panel of the Temple of the Cross, from Palenque (Chiapas): height, ca. 6 ft. Maya culture, Classic period, 6th-8th century A.D. The left panel of these famous slabs depicts a scene related to the corn cult, which shows two priests paying reverence to a cruciform symbol over which is seen a quetzal bird.

Lintel carved with scenes of offerings, from Yaxchilán (Chiapas): height, ca. 5 ft. 3 in. Maya culture, Classic period, 5th-8th century A.D. A priest, receiving homage and offerings, is carved on a door lintel in delicate relief. Hieroglyphic texts surround the figures.

Ball-game marker disk, from Cinkultic (Chiapas): diameter, ca. 21 ½ in. Maya culture, Classic period, 7th-8th century A.D.
The ritual ball game, played throughout ancient America by the Zapotecs as well as the Aztecs, was also played by the Maya.
Here, a ball player in the vestments of the game, is shown striking the ball with his hip. It was forbidden to touch it with
either hands or feet. The game was important as a demonstration of physical skill and force. As in ancient Greece, however,
athletics played an important role in religious, civil and military rituals which were linked with mathematics.

Adjacent to the museum, a full-scale reproduction of the main temple at Hochob (Campeche), the original dating from the 8th-9th century A.D., was reconstructed within a jungle setting. At the rear is a full-scale model of the temple at Bonampak (Chiapas)—originally dating from the 7th-9th century A.D.—whose three chambers contain a famous series of frescoes. In the center is a cast of the great stele of Quirigua, Guatemala. Guatemala, with Honduras, was the home of the Mayan heritage.

The mural frescoes of Bonampak are not only a treasure of art but also a mine of information about the ceremonies, life, ornaments, costumes, weapons, musical instruments, dances, techniques of war and many other aspects of Mayan life. Here three figures bedecked in bright colors and revealing the classic physiognomy of the Mayas, bring gifts to the high priest, who was generally also the supreme ruler.

as the Mayan. In addition to many imposing temples and stepped substructures, many specimens of the Mayas' civil architecture are extant. These civil-religious structures were used for certain ceremonial activities and also functioned as the dwellings of noble-priests, officials and other members of the population in general. The Mayas used the corbeled arch to roof a great number of still extant temples and palaces, and lined their buildings with stone blocks and slabs hewn with extraordinary skill and joined with mortar. Façades were profusely decorated with stones worked into countless varied motifs. The proportions and exceptional balance of these architectural masses impart to Mayan structures a unique effect of monumentality and harmony. The magnificent pyramidal structures of Tikal or Palenque, crowned by daring and elegant roofcombs, typify Mayan temple architecture. The so-called "Palace" of Palenque, with an elaborate system of inner courtyards bounded by long vaulted galleries, exemplifies Mayan dwellings, as does the majestic simplicity of the "Governor's Palace" at Uxmal.

Mayan sculpture, both in relief and in the round, is outstanding. Hundreds of slabs, lintels and stelae, apart from their undeniable aesthetic merit, depict an abundance of mythological and ceremonial scenes. These are accompanied by extensive hieroglyphic texts and chronological inscriptions, which provide an inexhaustible source for the study of the history and life of this people and their astonishing intellectual advances in astronomy, mathematics and time reckoning. Mathematics were the common base of Mayan society, politics and culture.

In the lapidary arts, jadeite was the material most frequently used to produce figurines, pectorals and a wide variety of other ornaments delicately carved in relief. The whimsical, eccentric flints of the Mayas, minutely worked by chipping and pressure flaking, and the inlaid disks of turquoise mosaic or other precious stones are brilliant technical feats of the post-Classic period of Chichén-Itzá. The Mayan sculptor worked other plastic materials such as stucco and fired clay with equally astonishing sensitivity. The finest examples of stucco work come from Palenque, which apparently was the center of this art.

Pottery underwent various phases of development in which many local styles were created. Particularly striking among the productions of the Classic period are the vessels and designs carved in relief or painted in bright polychrome, representing dignitaries, ceremonies, animals, abstract motifs and decorated glyphs. Large clay urns and cylinders were also decorated profusely with various baroque-like elements. The so-called "slate" pottery is a noteworthy example of sensitive design from the post-Classic period in Yucatán. Its elegant shape, decoration, texture and metallic finish reflect a high degree of technical proficiency. The terra-cotta figurines from the island of Jaina (Campeche) are world famous and have been favorably compared with the Tanagra figures of ancient Greece. Modeled with incomparable realism and charm, they display the physical type, dress, paraphernalia and customs of the Mayas of the sixth to the ninth century A.D. The pieces found among the funerary offerings of burials at Jaina and other sites on the Campeche coast are among the most admired relics of pre-Hispanic art.

The Mayas have also left magnificent examples of other modes of artistic expression, such as mural painting. The most important and admirable example of the pictorial arts encountered to date in any pre-Columbian civilization is the decorated walls of the three chambers of the Temple of Bonampak. Bonampak, discovered by the archaeologist Giles G. Healy in 1947 deep in the jungles of Chiapas, is Mayan for "painted walls." The paintings covering the walls of the three chambers develop in broad horizontal lines, one above the other. The theme of each chamber is different. The first depicts the investing of priests, a Mayan ceremony, with masked men dancing and musicians playing. Elsewhere in this fresco, several women are grouped about a throne, where a boy is being presented to dignitaries. The central chamber shows a battle in the jungle, and is followed by another showing the victorious Mayan warriors with a defeated enemy. These fresco paintings, a timeless example of the art of the most flourishing epoch of the pre-Hispanic world, also serve as a document which recounts a wealth of information about this ancient culture. Beauty of form, refinement, technical perfection and a high degree of intellectual achievement characterize the Mayan culture and make it without a doubt an important contribution to the arts of man everywhere.

A slave or captive, from Cumpich (Campeche): height, ca. 3 ft. Maya culture, 7th-10th century A.D. This remarkable naked figure of a prisoner, perhaps connected in some way with a fertility cult, stands against a full-scale model of the Temple of Hochob, placed in the gardens adjoining the Maya Room.

A notable, from Jaina (Campeche): height, ca. 10 ½ in. Maya culture, Classic period.

Athlete from Campeche: ca. 7 in. Maya culture, Classic period.

Mayan ruins are spread over southern Mexico, Guatemala, Honduras, British Honduras, and stretch as far as Costa Rica. At Bonampak, Uxmal or Palenque in Mexico, at Tikal in Guatemala, and at Copán in Honduras, are found the most remarkable sacred cities of one of the strangest civilizations the world has ever known. Among the rich

Ball players in various attitudes of the game, from Jaina (Campeche): height, ca. 5 and 6 in. Maya culture, Classic period.

Notables in elaborate headdress from Jaina (Campeche): height, ca. 6 ½ and 9 ½ in. Maya culture, Classic period.

Female figurines, from Jaina (Campeche): height, 7 ½ and 8 ½ in. Maya culture, Classic period.

sites of this culture are the Mayan cemeteries on the island of Jaina, opposite the Yucatán peninsula. There, from the 6th to the 9th century A.D., the Mayas buried with their dead thousands of images of their everyday life and religious customs. Learning, convention and sophistication became the attributes of Mayan life and culture.

Clay figures of old and sick people from Jaina (Campeche): height, ca. 6 to 6 ½ in. Maya culture, Classic period.

Weaver with loom from Jaina (Campeche): height, ca. 6 ½ in. Maya culture, Classic period.

Polychrome vase from Casas Grandes (Chihuahua): height, ca. 6 in. Culture of northern Mexico, 11th-12th century A.D. Imaginative geometric compositions with outstanding colors are skillfully integrated to form a bird of northern Mexico. Owing to the absence of rich flora, the decoration of the pottery of arid, desert-like northern Mexico tends to be abstract.

ART AND ARCHAEOLOGY OF NORTHERN MEXICO

They lived as hunters
Devoid of land and home
Wrapped not in woven cloak
But animal skin and plaited grass

ANNALS OF CUAUHITLÁN.

Most of the northern states of Mexico are located, geographically and ecologically, within what is called the "North American arid zone". The adverse climatic conditions that have prevailed in this region since pre-Hispanic times were a great obstacle to the economic and cultural development of its ancient peoples. For this reason, the northern cultures of Mexico are considered peripheral to the nucleus of high civilization that distinguished pre-Columbian Mesoamerica. In general, these were cultures of low technological and artistic level, developed by various nomadic or semi-sedentary groups. They managed to incorporate only partially some of the basic traits of the civilizations that flourished farther south.

More than ten thousand years ago bands of hunters of now extinct animals—representatives of the oldest people on the continent—gradually infiltrated the northern part of Mexico during their migrations toward the south. Isolated finds in the states of Lower California, Sonora, Chihuahua, Durango, Coahuila, Nuevo León and Tamaulipas have revealed the presence of these hunters of mammoths and bison. The disappearance of the Pleistocene animals through the ages caused a gradual change in the economy of these groups, slowly converting them into gatherers of wild fruits, tubers and grains. Archaeological sites in Sonora, northern Chihuahua and especially in Tamaulipas, have revealed materials belonging to this phase. During later periods—even up to the time of the European colonization of northern Mexico—the majority of these cultures remained almost static, in a state of precarious survival. Many of them have also been closely linked with various centers of similar cultures found in the south-western part of the United States as evidenced by the kinds and shapes of projectile points, and other carved-stone implements common to both regions. Two types of flint implements have been found in both culture areas; a small projectile point in the form of a leaf, and a larger knife-like instrument.

Apart from stonework, the material accomplishments of these peoples were very elementary. The catalogue of their art may be reduced to the numerous petroglyphs and outline paintings they left in rock shelters and on canyon walls. The most outstanding examples of this art have been discovered in certain remote areas of the peninsula of Lower California. These consist of large scenes depicting men and animals painted in brilliant colors and delineated in vigorous outline of surprising plastic merit. These paintings—as is believed to be the case with similar examples in other parts of the world—may have been created as an act of propitiatory magic, offered to gain success on hunting expeditions. Some of these rock paintings are very recent, later even than the Spanish colonization of the region in the sixteenth and seventeenth centuries, for in some cases motifs have been found that are not indigenous to the region, such as religious symbols, instruments, and images of domestic animals that became familiar in the area only after they had been introduced by the first European explorers and missionaries.

The pre-Columbian peoples of northern Mexico displayed great ability in working with wood to produce arms and utensils, as well as surprising technical ability in the manufacture of textiles from desert fibers. This is clearly demonstrated in the results obtained from the exploration of two caves, "La Candelaria" and "La Palia," which are of particular importance in the archaeological study of the whole north-western area of Mexico and the south-western United States. These two neighboring caves, located in the state of Coahuila, were excavated by Mexican archaeologists as recently as 1954. Both sites held an extraordinarily rich evidence of the local cultures, for their characteristic products, although made from perishable materials, were preserved in remarkably good condition owing to a climate that remained constant over several centuries. The implications of this preservation are quite important. Although the cultural products belong to a semi-nomadic people, whose cultural development was still to be realized, these products offer archaeologists the almost unique opportunity of studying cultures of a low degree of development in all their material aspects. This cannot be done with the great cultures of most of Mesoamerica, the study of which must generally be based upon objects made from non-perishable materials.

Both the "La Candeleria" and the "La Palia" caves were utilized between the twelfth and seventeenth centuries A.D. as burial grounds and funerary repositories; they must have been of primary importance. Hundreds of bodies in a flexed position were wrapped and buried in blankets made from regional vegetable fibers. Placed alongside the bodies were many funerary offerings, such as collars made from stone beads or vegetable seeds, bracelets woven with snake vertebrae, knives of carved stone with wooden, decorated handles, bows and arrows, nets, sandals and fiber bags, and many other kinds of bone, shell and wood ornaments. The advanced techniques shown in the manufacture of these instruments and artefacts is noteworthy.

Although reconstruction of these marginal cultures is by no means complete, there is sufficient evidence of their direct relation, as has already been said, with the advanced ceramic and agricultural cultures of the south-western United States. These cultures are the so called Anasazi, Mogollon and Hohokam. The Anasazi, whose name derives from a Navaho term meaning "the ancient ones," occupied north-eastern Arizona, north-western New Mexico and those areas that border upon each other of Colorado and Utah. Anasazi culture divides into two major periods, that of the Basket Maker Indians and that of the Pueblo period, the major development of which, between A.D. 1050 and 1300, witnessed the construction of the great cliff houses, such as at Mesa Verde, and advances in pottery craftsmanship, cotton and fiber weaving. The architectural plan of these dwellings as well as the pottery designs and weaving techniques show common elements with the cultures of north-western Mexico. The Hohokam, whose name derives from a Pima word meaning "those who have gone," occupied the southern half of Arizona and although they built individual rather than large community houses, they did excavate large areas that appear to have been ball courts such as are familiar in Mesoamerican cultures; even a rubber ball, such as the Maya used in their game, has been found in Hohokam territory. Their pottery also, particularly as it developed after A.D. 1100, shows an interest in designs and motifs similar to those found in north-western Mexico. Finally, the Mogollon, sharing with these cultures a certain contemporaneity and geographical location, relates to north-western Mexico. The Mogollon occupied territory east of the San Pedro river in Arizona. Again, pottery with skillful free-hand depictions of animal, insect and human forms, provides evidence for the relation of this culture to north-western Mexico.

This important archaeological area, of diverse peoples who overcame a difficult semi-desert environment to become sedentary, holds many things in common. They all began as cave-dwelling groups, they all hunted with the *atlatl* or spear-thrower, and they all evolved apartment-like constructions, similar pottery designs and weaving techniques. In the Sierra Madre range of Chihuahua and Sonora, for example, some constructions have been found in caves and rock shelters and against canyon walls that are evidently to be linked with the famous cliff dwellings of Utah, Colorado and Arizona. One of the largest and most important archaeological sites of northern Mexico is the ruins of Casas Grandes in Chihuahua. These ruins comprise a complex group of dwellings, ceremonial constructions and patios. Since they were built mainly of adobe, conservation has been difficult. Casas Grandes reached a peak during the tenth and eleventh centuries. The numerous burials excavated there, together with the finds of hundreds of pots and other funerary offerings, make this site the best-known in northern Mexico. The pottery is outstanding, employing motifs outlined in red and black, sharply contrasted with a cream-colored background.

Photomurals of archaeological ruins of the region provide background and atmosphere in the Northern Mexico Room. The buildings reproduced, enclosures of perishable adobe and cliff dwellings, indicate that the culture was on a very primitive level.

Model of cliff dwellings of Las Ventanas cave (Sierra Madre Occidental). Culture of northern Mexico, 11th-12th century A.D.

The cultures of Northern Mexico developed in a highly arid and primitive environment. Seen here are two models of dwellings typical of the region. The dwellings were generally built from adobe, with a wood frame-work. Adobe, a construction material still used in certain regions of Mexico and parts of Central and Southern America, is made from the amalgamation of wet mud and straw, formed into blocks and dried in the sun. Although fragile, this material hardens with age and is suited mainly for a dry, arid climate.

These constructions are of particular interest to students of the American Indian, since there are direct links between them and the well known cliff dwellings of the Anasazi, Mogollon and Hohokam Indians of the southwestern United States. In some cliff dwellings, such as the Las Ventanas cave seen above, many buried bodies were found accompanied by funerary offerings and ornaments of a fairly advanced design, ranging from bracelets of snake vertebrae to knives of carved stone.

Although similar structures can still be seen today in parts of Utah, Colorado and Arizona, little remains of the related structures of America's southern neighbors. The present-day Indians of this region of Mexico have changed their style of dwelling to thatched huts built on stick-work frames, that are among the most rudimentary of the Republic.

Clearly, therefore, one of the important areas of study of northern Mexico is the relationship of its sites and customs with those of its northern neighbors. Another extremely important area of exploration, however, is the relationship of these cultures with those that flourished further south. Some archaeological sites of significance in this connection are found along the northern border of Mesoamerica. Their principal value lies in the fact that they permit the study of the nature and sequence of cultural contacts and relationships between the north and central areas of Mexico in various periods. A noteworthy example is La Quemada in Zacatecas, with its imposing fortified structures and its elaborate pottery dome in a painted and incrusted decorative technique resembling *cloisonné*. Farther south the ruins of Toluquilla and Ranas also provide interesting examples of the architecture peculiar to that border area.

Recent field work in places such as Rio Verde, San Luis Potosí, Tunal Grande, Zacatecas, El Coparo, San Miguel de Allende and Guanajuato has further clarified the archaeology of those regions. The correct sequence of the cultures in this area can be determined in part by the occasional presence of well-known Mesoamerican implements, brought there perhaps by trade. An example of these is the typical yokes of the classical culture of El Tajín, which have been discovered in the northern part of Querétaro.

In sum, the ancient aboriginal cultures of northern Mexico, despite their marginal artistic and technological advances, constitute a rich field for anthropological research. Moreover, they provide an excellent opportunity for studying the mechanics of cultural transfer between the basically different groups that inhabited the arid regions of North America.

Model of a section of the archaeological city of Casas Grandes (Chihuahua). Culture of northern Mexico, 11th-12th century A.D. Several stories high, this group of ceremonial buildings had many rooms constructed with wood beams and adobe.

Pottery, from state of Durango: height, ca. 2½ to 7½ in. Culture of northern Mexico, Classic period, 11th-12th century A.D. Here are three examples of characteristic pottery shapes found in the northern periphery of this large culture area. The two vessels on the left are trade pieces from Sinaloa.

Polychrome ware with schematic decorations, from Casas Grandes (Chihuahua): height, ca. 5½ to 6½ in. Culture of northern Mexico, 11th-12th century A.D. The stylized facial expressions of sadness and surprise integrated into this type of geometric design on a cream-colored background are peculiar to Casas Grandes, and show a definite relationship to work from the southwestern part of the United States.

Anthropomorphic pot covers, from Coporo (northern Guanajuato): height, ca. 6½ in. Culture of northern Mexico, Late Classic period, 9th-11th century A.D. Traces of the influence of Teotihuacán and Hispanic cultures on northern Mexican pottery may be seen in these crude human representations, with headdresses that served as handles.

Hollow clay female figure, from Tequilia, Santiago Compostela (Nayarit): height, ca. 27 ½ in. Nayarit culture, Classic period, 8th-10th century A.D. Western Mexican clay sculpture consists nearly always of images of common men and simple everyday activities devoid of profound or abstruse symbolic and religious intent. This figure of a Nayarit woman in the position of giving birth is one of the most beautiful art works of that culture.

ART AND ARCHAEOLOGY OF WESTERN MEXICO

Every moon, every year,
Every day, every wind,
Comes and is gone.
All blood, too, reaches
Its place of quietness.

CHILAM BALAM.

A great culture area vaguely designated in anthropological literature as the "area of the Western cultures," covers an extensive portion of western Mexico, which encompasses the southern part of the state of Sinaloa in the north and most of the state of Guerrero in the south. The lack of knowledge of the origins, chronology and development of the pre-Hispanic peoples who inhabited this territory is reflected in the very vagueness of the name applied to it. However, even though scientifically controlled archaeological excavations in this region have so far been few, despite its obvious importance and wealth of material, thousands of archaeological pieces have been found, and for decades pieces, particularly from Jalisco, Colima, Nayarit and Guerrero, have accumulated in museums, art galleries and private collections in Mexico and other countries. Although these represent some of the best known pre-Hispanic art styles, they have yet to be grounded on a solid base of research.

Western Mexico may, to a certain extent, be considered marginal to the cultural flowering of the rest of pre-Hispanic Mesoamerica. Village-type cultures that developed various regional styles covered most of this territory. These cultures, which began in pre-Classic times and survived well into our era, have remained almost totally static neither originating nor assimilating any significant technological or intellectual advances. The archaeology of Jalisco, Colima and Nayarit is distinguished by almost total absence of certain cultural elements (such as monumental architecture and stone sculpture) which reached such a high stage of development in other parts of Mesoamerica. Writing and the calendar were completely unknown. These may be categorized as essentially ceramic cultures, in view of the fact that their creations in this medium are of surprising quality and diversity.

Two of the best-known pre-Classic sites of western Mexico are El Opeño in Michoacán and Chupicuaro in Guanajuato. Extensive excavations carried out some years ago by the National Museum of Anthropology, particularly in Chupicuaro, uncovered a rich harvest of materials from these ancient cultures. Numerous burials yielded hundreds of extraordinary clay vessels and figurines of a unique style. Chupicuaro ceramics of the Late pre-Classic phase are outstanding in variety of form; their finely finished burnished surfaces are predominantly red, black, white and buff in color.

The Jalisco, Colima and Nayarit styles, each so strongly individual, did not develop until the Classic period. An enormous quantity of hollow clay sculpture was produced, exhibiting great freedom in the modeling and the attitudes of the human figures. Representations of men, women and children carrying out the most varied activities of daily life constitute an ethnographical document of inestimable value for reconstructing the lives and customs of these peoples. Clay models of their houses, temples and ball courts are equally important documents. The hollow effigies of parrots, rabbits, armadillos, fish, crabs and other animals from Colima are particularly charming. The famous fattened dog figures, hairless dogs bred for food, are especially prized among the archaeological pieces of Mexico.

This rich ceramic hoard from Jalisco, Colima and Nayarit seems to be funerary in origin and comes from the shaft tombs with underground chambers that are scattered throughout the region. El Arenal in Jalisco and Ixtlán del Rio in Nayarit are two of the few sites even moderately well studied to date. One of the rare examples of architecture of this culture area was found at the latter site; this construction, dating from the end of the Classic period, is circular in shape and shows Teotihuacán influence.

Little is known about the early phases of the state of Michoacán; only a moderate amount of material from the Apatzingán region and El Opeño has been available for study. Information begins with the centuries immediately preceding the Spanish Conquest, during which the Tarascan civilization consolidated its control over a broad territory, and established its main centers in the lake region of Michoacán. The Tarascans, who developed a highly diversified and very individual culture, were among the few groups of Mesoamerica to successfully resist the onslaughts of powerful Aztec militarism from central Mexico. Their main ceremonial centers were Tzintzuntzán and Ihuatzio, on the shores of Lake Pátzcuaro. They built large religious constructions of an extremely unusual type, known as "yacatas," which were raised on top of gigantic platforms and were laboriously built with closely fitted plain slabs of volcanic stone. In these unusual constructions, semi-circular masses were placed at regular intervals against a rectangular stepped structure.

A few notable examples of Tarascan stone sculpture are known. Pieces such as the Chac-Mool, a great reclining figure, a couple embracing or the effigy of a coyote exhibited in the Tarascan section of the Museum are exceptional manifestations of sculptural form in nearly geometric terms. Tarascan ceremonial pottery is distinguished by its brilliant red, yellow, white and black polychrome decoration. Vessels of extraordinary and elegant shape, decorated with handles or sharp protuberances serving as spouts or handles are quite frequent. Delicately modeled and painted miniature vases are equally frequent. The Tarascans also excelled in fashioning gold, silver, copper and precious stones into works of art. They worked obsidian with incredible skill, reducing this brittle volcanic stone nearly to the thinness of paper. They manufactured from it delicate earrings and many other ornaments which were further embellished with gold, mosaics or turquoise.

Another practically unknown cultural area of western Mexico is the mountainous state of Guerrero. A few isolated sites which have been recently explored indicate that this territory has very particular archaeological interest and may indeed harbor the solution to many unsolved mysteries of the Mesoamerican past. This vast region has been occupied for many centuries since very early times and appears to have been the crucible in which many different cultures mixed and fused, with the Olmec culture evidently having been of particular importance. The archaeology of Guerrero, like that of most of western Mexico, is known on the basis of the more or less arbitrary definition of artistic "styles" characteristic of given areas. An abundance of these materials, either accidental finds or uncontrolled excavations, are in museums and private collections. The best known style of Guerrero is the so-called Mezcala culture of the Balsas River basin. Distinguished for its high level of development in the working of serpentine and other semi-precious stones, the Mezcala style is especially prized by students of pre-Hispanic art because of the vigorous stylization of the countless human and animal figures.

Aspects of the cultures of western Mexico, particularly of Jalisco, Colima and Nayarit, are not often manifested in other pre-Hispanic civilizations and are recorded almost solely by their clay sculpture. Because of the relatively marginal nature of their cultures, the invaluable records left by these peoples have enabled us to reconstruct, if only partially, their daily lives and domestic activities. Such civilizations as the Aztec, Maya, Teotihuacán and Zapotec are known largely through their public, religious and ceremonial manifestations, which by their very nature were restricted to selective moments in the lives of a privileged minority of the population. In western Mexico, on the contrary, the life of the common man has been made known through the simple, amiable art he created in an atmosphere relatively free of religious strictures.

Chac-Mool, from Ihuatzio (Michoacán): length, ca. 56½ in., height, ca. 33½ in. Tarascan culture, 13th-16th century A.D. Two of the ▶ few existing pieces of Tarascan stone sculpture are this outstanding image of Chac-Mool and that of a coyote, skillfully stylized through the use of geometric planes. The idea of the reclining Chac-Mool was imported from the Mesoamerican cultures of the central highlands.

Hollow clay figure, from state of Nayarit: height, ca. 22 in. Culture of western Mexico, Classic period, 8th-10th century A.D. The figure of a man sitting on a chair is formed from ▼ one piece of clay, with ingenuity and forceful stylization.

Warrior or ball player, from Jalisco: height, ca. 17 ½ in. Jalisco culture, Classic period, 7th-10th century A.D. This man has a helmet, chest and leg protectors, and holds a club.

Sitting clay figure from the state of Colima: height, ca. 8½ in. Culture of Western Mexico, Classic period, 8th-10th century A.D. Men and women are often shown in a variety of poses and everyday appearance, as is this man.

Hunchback on a two-headed fish, from the state of Colima: height, ca. 16¼ in. Colima culture, Classic period, 7th-10th century A.D. An old man, with perforated ear-lobes, stands on a two-headed fish and leans against a stick. ▼

Clay family group, from state of Colima: height, ca. 7 in. Colima culture, Classic period, 8th-10th century A.D. The importance of family life is well represented in this group.

Water carrier from the state of Colima: height, ca. 9 in. Colima culture, Classic period, 7th-10th century A.D. This clay sculpture of a bearer demonstrates the power of stylization of human characteristics the Colima artists possessed.

Pot adorned with human heads, from state of Colima: height, ca. 7 in. Culture of western Mexico, 7th-8th century A.D. These commonly used circular pots were variously decorated with human, bird or animal heads or with vegetable motifs.

Vase in *cloisonné* technique from Jiquilpán (Michoacán): height, ca. 15 ½ in. Tarascan Classic period, 7th-8th century A.D.

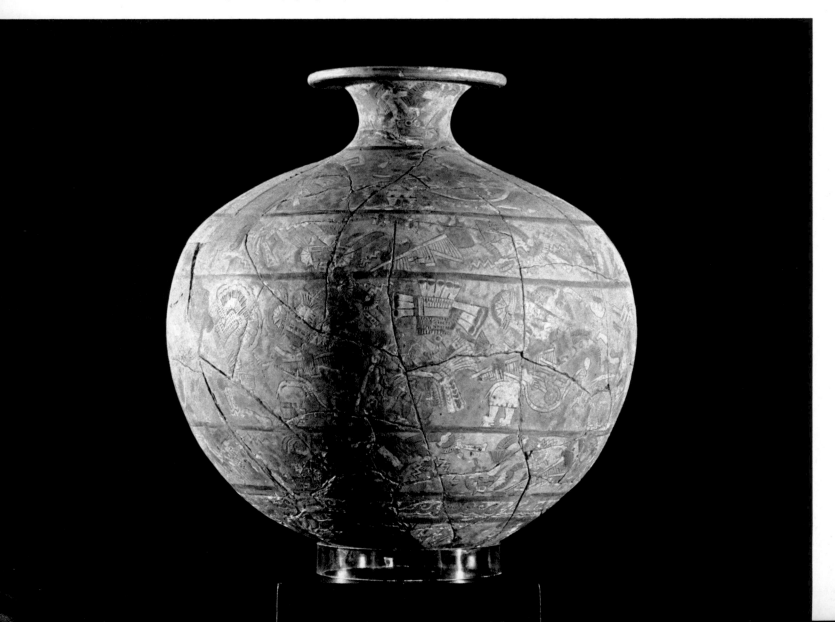

Large-eared clay mouse and dog with his feet in the air, from state of Colima: length, 12 ½ and 9 ½ in. Colima culture, Classic period, 8th - 10th century A.D. These two animals served as vases.

Characteristic of the pottery of the Classic period of Colima are these playful and plastically interesting representations of common animals, particularly the *itzcuintli*, hairless dogs that served as food and were also rendered in the shape of jugs and pots. The culture of Colima, as distinct from that of Nayarit and Jalisco, has fewer pre-Classic characteristics. Sculptures are of terra-cotta, in shades running from cream to brown, and are occasionally painted a reddish brown and red. Subject matter is surprisingly varied, and both human and animal forms are habitually treated with realism. Common animals and men and women, shown in a variety of everyday activities, are depicted with affection and often with happy and even joyous expressions.

Clay parrot from the state of Colima: height, ca. 8 in. Colima culture, Classic period, 8th-10th century A.D.

Howling dog from the state of Colima: height ca. 9 in. Colima culture, Classic period, 8th-10th century A.D.

173

Clay female figure from Jalisco: height ca. 12 in.   Jalisco culture, Classic period, 7th-10th century A.D.
This squatting contemplative figure, found in a tomb where it was left as a funerary offering, is
known as "The Venus of Western Mexico."   Her head was perhaps deformed for purposes of beauty.

Terra-cotta female figurine from state of Colima: height, 16 ½ in. Culture of western Mexico, Classic period, 8th-10th century A.D. This figure of a seated woman is notable for its prominent torso, marked facial features, and short arms. She also wears typical ornaments on her shoulders.

Terra-cotta house group from Ixtlán (state of Nayarit): height, ca. 7 in. This scene, with various figures inside and outside the typical house, gives eloquent and simple testimony of life in this culture, which is quite similar today.

IV.   THE ETHNOLOGY OF MEXICO

Shall I depart as the flowers that withered?
Will anything remain of my name?
Nothing of my name here on earth!
At least my flowers, at least my songs!

SONGS OF HUETZINGO.

All the peoples of the Americas, north and south, are immigrants or descendants of immigrants. The most familiar and widely known Americans are, of course, people who came to this continent within the last five hundred years. But even the Indians, who are surely less generally or familiarly known, and whom we think of as native, were also immigrants. America was once a new world to all the groups now living in the hemisphere.

There is little doubt that the increasingly exact study and widespread recognition of the Indian's active role, past and present, in Mexico's culture is part of a revolution in self-consciousness that Latin America is undergoing in this century. It is a revolution that may be observed in several Central American countries and in several South American nations like Bolivia, Peru, Ecuador or Chile. But this revolution for the integration of diverse elements in a nation has its parallels elsewhere on the continent—the French in Canada, the Negro and other minority groups in the United States, for example. And because it does, the study of how Mexico has incorporated its Indian population into contemporary life and culture is bound to be instructive to any other people on the hemisphere.

But we must go on to note that as more and more Indian groups are absorbed into contemporary culture, the Indian traditions surviving in Mexico are threatened with disappearance. However, the costumes, artefacts, dwellings and customs of the major Indian groups have been preserved for posterity in the National Museum of Anthropology. In this section of the book, photographs of the indigenous peoples of Mexico are contrasted with the museum exhibits, producing a juxtaposition which not only carries out the museum's function of preserving the past but also gives a rich panorama of Mexico today. This is indeed the essential and comprehensive purpose of the museum. It not only offers the visitor of whatever cultural origin or affiliation a visual understanding of what Indian Mexico is like, but equally important it gives the native Indian himself the means by which to see himself in relation to his own ancestors. In effect, and without the slightest condescension, the pre-Columbian past, in all its human drama and historical order, is created before the very eyes of the Indian visitor. The Nahuatl poet, quoted above, feared the mortality of his race even before the coming of the Spanish conquerors. But he had faith in the immortality of his "song," the theme and melody of his poetry, and in his "flowers," the metaphors and analogies inherent in the power of words. The native visitor to the museum makes it clear that the Indian has survived as a person; the museum makes it clear that he has also survived in the strength of his past.

Mexico's indigenous peoples are descended from Mongoloid groups that reached the American continent by way of the Bering Strait about 25,000 B.C., during the geological period just preceding the present

◄ A young couple, shown on their wedding day, are representative of the indigenous cultures of Mexico. The traditional wedding dress is still worn by the women of Jamiltepec, a small Mixtec village on the coast of Oaxaca. On this day the bride is first permitted to wear earrings and to cover her head with a *huipil*. The bridegroom wears the typically Indian costume of rough cotton trousers and blouse.

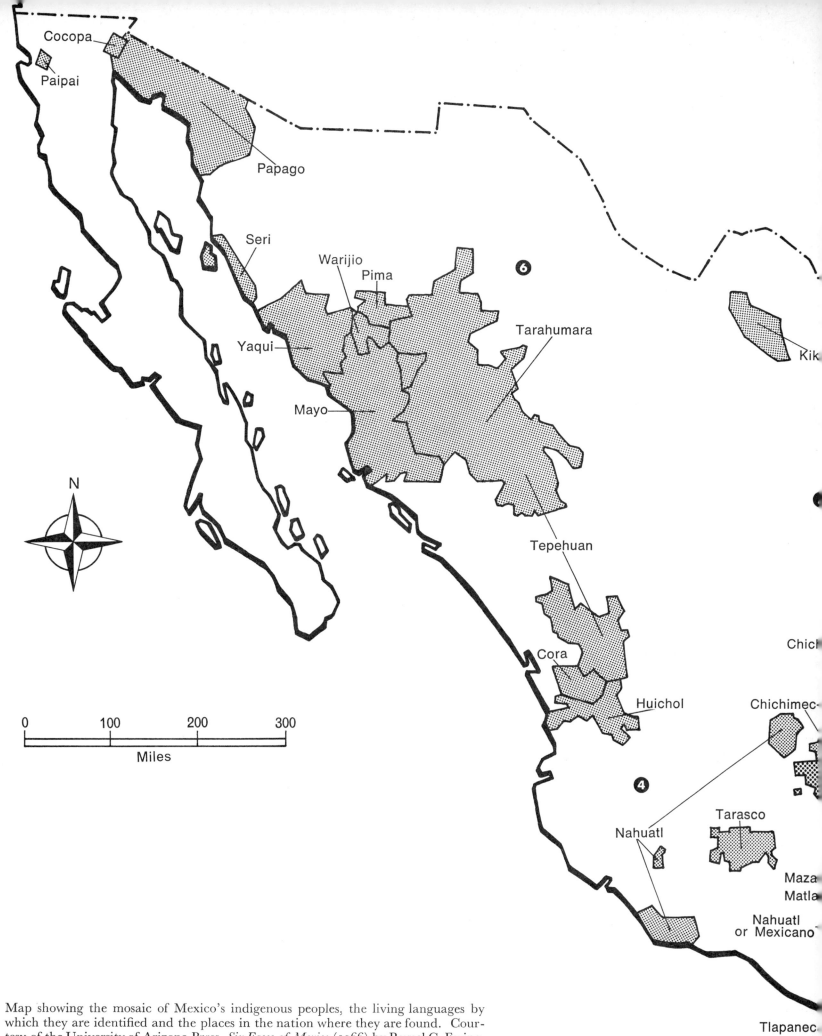

Cocopa

Paipai

Papago

Seri

Warijio

Pima

Yaqui

Tarahumara

Mayo

❻

Kik

Tepehuan

Cora

Chich

Huichol

Chichimec-

❹

Tarasco

Nahuatl

Maza
Matla

Nahuatl
or Mexicano

N

0   100   200   300
Miles

Map showing the mosaic of Mexico's indigenous peoples, the living languages by
which they are identified and the places in the nation where they are found. Courtesy of the University of Arizona Press, *Six Faces of Mexico* (1966) by Russel C. Ewing.

Tlapanec

Principal Indian Languages

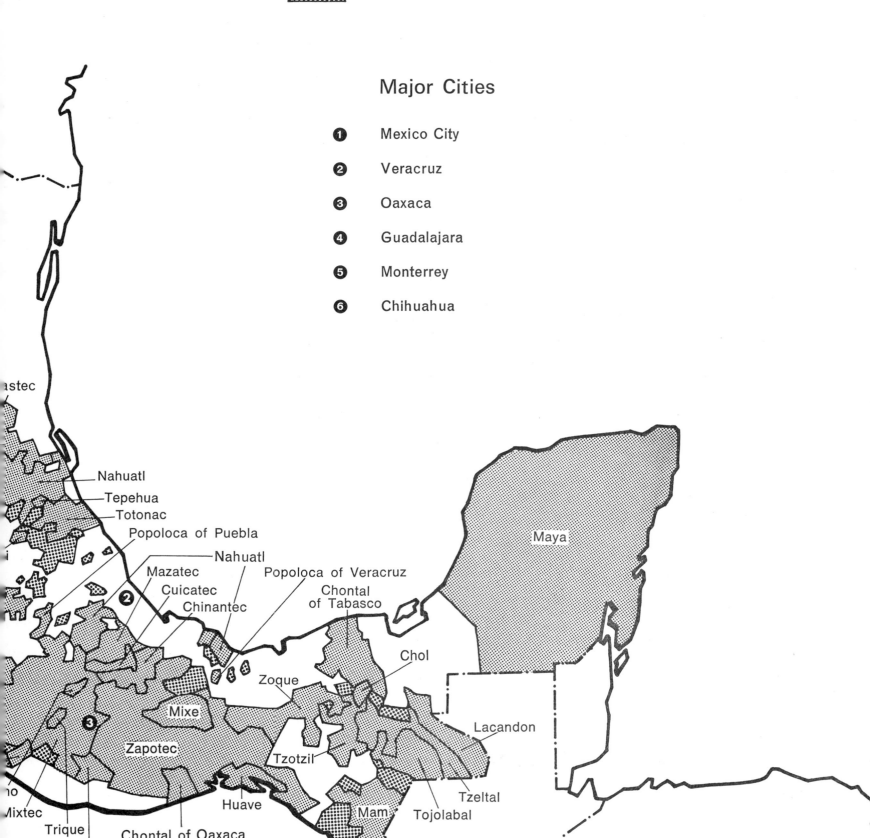

Major Indian Language Groups

Other Indian Language Groups

Major Cities

1 Mexico City

2 Veracruz

3 Oaxaca

4 Guadalajara

5 Monterrey

6 Chihuahua

astec

Nahuatl

Tepehua

Totonac

Popoloca of Puebla

Nahuatl

Mazatec

Popoloca of Veracruz

Cuicatec

Chinantec

Chontal
of Tabasco

Maya

Chol

Zoque

Mixe

Lacandon

Zapotec

Tzotzil

Mixtec

Huave

Tzeltal

Mam

Tojolabal

Trique

Chontal of Oaxaca

Chatino

one. They scattered throughout the American continent, and large numbers settled in Mesoamerica, an area stretching from northern Mexico to southern Honduras. It is in this territory that the major pre-Columbian civilizations flourished, as seen in the earlier section of this book.

The cultures of the Mesoamerican Indians, despite their differences, had many things in common. For example, pyramid-like constructions, a solar and ritual calendar, the belief in many gods, known by different names but essentially constituting one pantheon, and many common arts and crafts. Much of this heritage is preserved by contemporary Indian groups in altered forms, to be sure, for it is plain that neither languages nor other forms of Indian life and culture, are today what they were immediately before the Conquest. Change and alteration are a constant of all human life and the history of any country causes changes in its traditions, however adaptable these may be.

When the Spaniards arrived, there probably were some twenty-five million people in the territory of present-day Mexico. They spoke some one hundred and eighty different languages, some of which had from four or five to twelve dialects. Many Indians still display, despite age-old and varied mixtures, the physical characteristics of their ancestors: straight, dark hair, scant hair on face or body, brown skin and dark eyes. Such features as height, and shape of head and nose, vary considerably, of course, but they may be used to identify subtypes. The Indians of the northwest, for example, are usually tall, well-proportioned and long-headed, while those of the central highlands are shorter, round-headed, and broad of nose. In the south these characteristics become even more pronounced.

Indians and Spaniards intermarried and originated the Mexican mestizo. Intermarriage was not limited to these two groups, however, for it also took place with Negro slaves brought from Africa during the sixteenth and seventeenth centuries. During the Colonial period, for administrative and civic purposes, the Spanish authorities divided the population into "castes" according to the types and degrees of mixture in each inhabitant. The principal castes were the mestizo, a descendant of Spaniard and Indian, and the castiza or descendant of Spaniard and mestizo. For political reasons a descendant of the castiza caste was again considered a Spaniard and enjoyed equal rights with him, a fact which was not reflected by any other kind or degree of mixture among the races present in Colonial Mexico.

During the Colonial period neither Spaniards nor Negroes were allowed to live in Indian communities, but this measure, partly protective and partly restrictive, was unenforceable in the areas surrounding the Spanish centers. With the winning of independence after 1810, these systems were abolished, and the Indians were guaranteed exclusive use of their communal lands. Many, however, sold their land to whites and to mestizos, initiating the infiltration of outsiders into Indian villages and eventually causing the creation of "regions of refuge," a term invented by Gonzalo Aguirre Beltrán. However underdeveloped an outsider may consider these regions, they have served to protect the uniqueness of Indian cultures. Other groups, because of geographic isolation, remained almost untouched.

Because of the many varieties and degrees of racial mixture, the definition of the term Indian in today's context presents a number of difficulties. Traditionally, the definition begins with the languages he speaks. Very many Indian languages are spoken in contemporary Mexico—more than forty-three, in fact—and it is possible that continuing linguistic studies will increase this number. These languages constitute four linguistic groups: the Maya-Totonac group, including exclusively Mesoamerican tongues spoken mainly in southern Mexico; the Otomanguean group of central Mexico and Oaxaca; the Nahua-Cuitlatec group of central and northwestern Mexico; and the southern Hokan group, used on the Pacific coast. Maya-Totonac comprises several stocks that include the Totonac, Mixean, Tarascan and the Mayan languages spoken in southern Mexico and Guatemala, among them the Maya of the peninsula proper and the Lacandon and Tzeltal-Tzotzil of Chiapas. The Otomanguean group also includes various stocks; Otopame, Mixtec, Zapotec and Chinantecan are the best known. The Nahua-Cuitlatec group is the most important of the four in both extent and number of speakers, for in addition to Nahua proper it also includes such northwestern languages as Tarahumara and Cora-Huichol. To the Hokan group belong the languages of Indians spread out along the Pacific coast, such as the Seris of Sonora

History is visible in a Mexican's face. After centuries of intermarriage, it is notable how the features of the ancient pre-Hispanic peoples of Mexico are still distinctly seen in the face and body types of the nation's contemporary inhabitants. There is a parallel continuity in the style of dress for men and women. Seen here are four different ethnic types, each typical of its kind in physical appearance and dress: from Puebla (*lower left*); from the Cuicatec region of Oaxaca (*upper right*); from the Chinantla zone of Oaxaca (*center right*); and a Seri woman from northwestern Mexico (*below right*).

and the Tlapanec of Guerrero. Some one hundred and eighty languages were spoken in Mexico when the Spaniards arrived. In 1960, according to the census, about 3,030,000 Mexicans over five years of age spoke indigenous languages, either as their only language or with another language or Spanish. The total population of Mexico was about 34,700,000; hence, indigenous peoples constituted somewhat less than ten percent of the total. Although the Indian population has increased by about 800,000 since 1960, it now accounts for a smaller percentage of the total.

These statistics provide a reasonably accurate index to the number of persons identifiable as indigenous groups, but they do not necessarily indicate a low degree of "acculturation," or cultural assimilation. Particularly among largely bilingual groups, preservation of the traditional tongue does not imply rejection or isolation from modern culture. And conversely, Indians who speak Spanish and wear Western clothing may still follow basically Indian patterns of life. Despite its diversity, language has been and still is a decisive factor in the persistence of group identity among indigenous peoples. Through it the personality, values and world view of the group survive and are strengthened.

Today, geographically, the indigenous population of Mexico is widely spread and surprisingly stable. Twenty-three of the thirty-two states and territories of the republic have Indian groups or nuclei of some size, and in the southern and central portions the concentration is quite heavy. The Maya of the Yucatán Peninsula and the state of Chiapas constitute the largest single unified group; the states of Oaxaca, Puebla, Veracruz, Mexico and Hidalgo also have large groups of Indians, and smaller concentrations live in Guerrero, San Luis Potosí, Michoacán and Chihuahua. Often these indigenous peoples occupy regions of refuge, which generally surround villages and are intimately related to them. These villages may dominate their "colonies," but they are often almost as backward as the regions themselves.

Indigenous characteristics have survived among many Indian groups because these peoples have had little or no contact with other cultures and have therefore not benefited by acculturation. Many Indians, however, are more or less integrated into the main stream of Mexican life, either "spontaneously," because they live near and work in major urban centers, or because their acculturation has been planned by social scientists, mainly social and applied anthropologists, and carried out through regional programs and through the National Indigenous Institute. The Institute attempts to acculturate isolated Indian groups by working both with the Indians and the mestizos inhabiting the "regions of refuge," in order to alter and improve the relationship between them. The Institute sponsors Coordinating Centers in the nucleus towns, which attempt to change Indian life according to an established plan, respecting the indigenous cultural values, yet convincing the Indian of the advantages to be had by participating in the national culture. These programs have met with considerable success, as in the Tarascan community of Pátzcuaro.

Language and physical characteristics thus help to identify the Indian. But collective forms of art and dress, of religion and government also provide elements of identity. And beyond observable phenomena of this kind, there are others accessible only to understanding: the indigenous peoples are bound together by a strong egocentrism which both preserves and is preserved by their culture. Similar ideals of beauty, a common metaphysical outlook, food based upon an essentially agricultural economy, often cooked by methods centuries old, social structures ranging from endogamy to elaborate systems of lineage and class, religious practices that combine Indian with Christian elements, as well as types of feminine and masculine wear, all make the Indian groups distinctive and tend to keep them separate from the national culture. Mexico is thus a mosaic of different cultures.

Perhaps one of the strongest barriers separating the Indian from the national culture is the tightly knit organization of the Indian village, where traditional Indian and Spanish forms of government survive. Civil and religious posts are closely connected and carry considerable status. Often men devote a great deal of time and money to serving the community in various offices; eventually many attain the position of *anciano* (elder) or *principale* (chief). As such they are part of a highly respected and ultra-conservative advisory group which protects the harmony between the town and the universe around it—preventing drought and sickness and ensuring good crops by the invocation of ancient gods and Catholic saints.

Two years of intensive nation-wide photographing produced the largest record to date of the Indians of Mexico, which has become a substantial part of the ethnographic exhibitions of the museum. This introductory showcase unites the present with the past by showing that certain physical characteristics are as common in the Indians of today as they were in those of yesterday. Their facial characteristics are similar—coarse, straight, dark hair, yellow-brown skin, slanted brown eyes, prominent cheekbones, thick lips, and strong, white teeth—while they differ in stature. In northwestern Mexico, Indians like the Seri and Yaqui are tall and well proportioned, whereas in the southeast they are short-legged, small in stature, and broadheaded.

Civil posts may be elective, but a man must be appointed to a religious post. As a custodian of one of the Catholic saints, for example, he cares for the image throughout the year and arranges celebrations for the feast-day. Each custodian hopes that his festival will be the most splendid, and all his family works to make it so. An elaborate banquet is prepared, everyone wears his best clothing, and visitors come from nearby villages to parade through the church and to see rockets and displays of fireworks. These festivals combine music, dances, and rituals of pre-Hispanic origin with the rites of the Catholic church; in many places, indeed, the two religious traditions are completely integrated. Everyone wears new suits on this day; for several days before all the women in the custodian's family will have been grinding corn for the banquet, which will be attended by all the town's authorities, in strict order of protocol. The day before, all the visitors come from the nearby hamlets and towns to enjoy the rockets and fireworks display, but always after first parading through the church which has been decorated with flowers and candles. Street vendors also appear, as do sideshows, such as merry-go-rounds and shooting stalls and other games, and the mestizos of the town set up their food stalls. On the same day as the fiesta, dances are staged by the young people of the town accompanied by the town musicians. Then comes the banquet and the fiesta ends with a mass, celebrated by at least three priests, if possible. With this the custodian's duties are at an end and this same day he relinquishes the image of the saint to the next custodian. The custodian and his wife have fulfilled their duty and have gained the esteem of all who are aware of the sacrifices they have made; the fiesta will have cost them from 8,000 to 10,000 pesos ($650-$850) and they have undoubtedly been forced to go into debt or sell part of their land in order to perform this duty in a proper manner.

The indigenous peoples of Mexico inherited a rich artistic tradition. Their Spanish conquerors found monumental sculpture and painting, sophisticated architecture, and highly developed minor arts—jade carving, gold work, mosaic—connected with religious and court life. These artistic traditions did not long remain untouched, but even today, in remote areas, some Indian groups practice the arts of their forebears—ancient Mixtec painting, for example, and the feather mosaics of the Tarascans. Throughout Mexico, what has survived of these traditions is maintained by the Indian women, who were, and often still are, the weavers and potters. Lacquerwork still flourishes in Michoacán and Guerrero, and the making of musical instruments, incense burners for household altars, masks, and other ritual accoutrements are crafts in themselves. The Indian past is thus still a potent constant in Mexican life.

In many regions, the making of pottery most faithfully carries on ancient traditions, techniques and styles. Clay is prepared according to traditional methods, and the form of vessels remains the same. Much pottery is not glazed but polished by hand or decorated with slip or incised designs. In some villages the visitor may buy the zoomorphic jugs used to carry water from the sacred spring. In addition to producing pottery by traditional methods, Indian craftsmen now use molds, glazes, and other European techniques, especially for ware to be sold to the urban mestizo population and to tourists from abroad.

Contemporary Indian dress is extremely rich and varied. Women wear such purely indigenous garments as the *huipil*, the *quechquemitl* (a poncho or smock), and the *enredo* (a wraparound skirt), as well as mestizo garments like the *rebozo* and the embroidered blouse and skirt. The materials used vary with the region: certain Otomi groups use *ixtle*, the fiber of the maguey plant; white and brown cotton is used in Oaxaca, and wool in the mountain regions. The *quechquemitl* is worn throughout Mexico, from the Gulf Coast to the Western Sierra Madre. Much clothing of pre-Hispanic origin is woven on the backstrap loom, but some, like the brocaded gauze of the Cuetzalán *quechquemitl*, involves complex weaving and dyeing techniques, each of them indicative of pride in skill and origin.

Most Indian men wear mestizo dress: muslin shirts and trousers, hats, and *huaraches* (sandals). Two traditional garments have survived: the *maxtlatl*, a loincloth now transformed into a sash, and the *manta* (mantle), adapted into the *serape*. The only pre-Hispanic article of clothing that has survived intact is the long bark-cloth tunic worn by the Lacandons in religious ceremonies. Among many groups the style of dress is so distinctive that it is possible to identify a person's village by the cut of his garment or the way in which he wears it. A man's position as an official of his village is also reflected in his clothing.

Modern Mexicans take great pride in the indigenous aspects of their country. They consider the Indian traditions an important and especially rich part of their cultural heritage, yet many are unaware of the precarious reality in which the inhabitants of the "regions of refuge" live. Mexico's rich indigenous cultures distinguish it from other nations; indeed, if Mexico were to project its cultural message to the world, it would be the indigenous peoples and traditions that would make it unique.

The most important aspects of the material culture of the Indians of Mexico in all its sensitivity, artistic imagination, and creative vigor are presented in the Introduction to Ethnography Room. The figures on the left illustrate the making of Indian dresses; the women beat the cotton, spin the thread on a spindle whorl, and weave the cloth on a hip loom, just as they did before the Conquest. On the right is a Nahua granary of Tetelcinco, Morelos. In the cases in the background are instruments for hunting and fishing, and a wide variety of handicrafts, including lacquerwork boxes and gourds from Olinalá, deep trays and pottery from Michoacán, and many *ixtle* and palm-leaf objects. This is the principal exhibition room on the second floor.

CORA-HUICHOL ETHNOGRAPHY

REGION. The Cora and Huichol Indians occupy the Sierra de Nayarit, a section of the Eastern Sierra Madre that rises north of the Rio Grande de Santiago and includes the eastern part of Nayarit State, where the Cora live, and the northwestern part of Jalisco, homeland of the Huichol Indians. The region is crossed from north to south by large rivers with many tributaries, which cut through deep canyons bordered by cliffs and peaks. Among these mountains, at an altitude ranging from 5,000 to 6,500 feet above sea level, are valleys and plateaus covered with coniferous forests and pasture land. The Cora Indians number around 4,000 and the Huichol some 7,000.

LANGUAGE. The languages of both the Cora and Huichol Indians are of the Uto-Azteca linguistic family. Among the Huichol there are small local language variants in the communities of San Andres, Santa Catarina, and San Sebastian.

HISTORY. Because they inhabited impenetrable mountains, the Cora and Huichol Indians escaped the Conquest and the subsequent rebellions that ravaged the western part of Mexico during the sixteenth and seventeenth centuries. Later, defending themselves against soldiers and priests, they preserved their independence until 1721, mainly through the fierce resistance of the Cora Indians. In 1721 and 1722 they were conquered, and the colonial government installed garrisons and missions in their territory. In 1767, after the expulsion of the Jesuits, the area recovered some of its independence, mainly in the Huichol region. From that time on they remained very isolated.

ECONOMY. Being close neighbors, the Cora and Huichol Indians share many cultural traits, among them their economy, which is principally agricultural. Because of their timid and very emotional nature, the Huichol Indians have always maintained their traditional, isolated way of life, and with it the handicrafts by which they augment their economy. The arrogant and rebellious Cora Indians, however, are practical and innate merchants, and they have abandoned handicrafts to devote themselves to livestock breeding and the manufacture of commercial articles.

HANDICRAFTS AND DRESS. The Huichol Indians produce various handicrafts, as may be seen in their color-ful attire. The men wear long-tailed, white, coarse cotton shirts belted with sashes, which hang down over white, coarse cotton trousers, and small capes bordered with red flannel. Hanging down from the sashes is a row of richly embroidered bags joined to each other. Their wide-brimmed, double palm-leaf hats are decorated to suit the occasion. This gala dress is complemented by elaborate earrings, bracelets, and necklaces made of blue and white beading. Almost all the Huichol Indians carry a small homemade

◄ The Huichol culture, one of the simplest in the country because of its geographic isolation in the Sierra de Nayarit, has managed to main-tain great continuity in its arts and dress. These Huichol men wear long-tailed cotton shirts belted with sashes, and white cotton trousers.

A typical Huichol house of one windowless room is made from stone and mud and has a thatched roof. The kitchen and corn crib are outside. The Huichol Indians remain on their farms, where the men share the work and the women grind corn, prepare food, and weave. Much interdependence exists among the Huichol Indians, who form a tightly knit economic unit.

violin in a carrying bag. In contrast, the women's dress is simple, consisting of coarse cotton long-sleeved blouses, and skirts that hang down to the ankles. Especially during religious festivals, they cover their heads with a cotton square or triangle, and some wear a *quechquemitl* bordered with fretwork and bead necklaces. The Huichols make small pieces of furniture and fashion gourds to store tobacco. They carve rough idols from soapstone and make beautiful votive offerings for the gods.

DWELLING. The typical house of the region is the thatched hut; it is surrounded by smaller huts, which are the individual shrines of gods. At the head of each community is a *casa real* (royal house) made of adobe and stone. It has a long corridor with a rough altar surrounded by Catholic saints. Here important ceremonies and assemblies are held. Other huts house the authorities when they come to the chief village, and there is a house for the *mayordomo* (religious steward), and sometimes a small tent. Twenty-two temples have been built near sacred caves in which the Indian deities are believed to live; these are elliptical and have thatched roofs. There is also a great temple called *casa grande* (great house), around which is a series of small shrines with rough clay altars on which offerings are placed.

RELIGION. The destiny of the Huichol Indians is ruled by more than forty principal deities, the majority of which are related to the agricultural cycle. Among the masculine gods are those of the dry season like *Padre Sol* (Father Sun), head god of San Andres; *Abuelo Fuego* (Grandfather Fire), head deity of Santa

188

Catarina; *Bisabuelo Cola de Venado* (Great-grandfather Deer) of San Sebastian; and the *Estrella de la Mañana* (Morning Star). Of greater importance in daily life are the gods of water, headed by *Nakawe* or *Abuela Crecimiento* (Grandmother Growth). There is also a goddess of maize and four gods of rain who preside over the growth of plants. The *casa grande* and the sacred caves are the site for fifteen great festivals each year. In these the ritual, directed by a chanting shaman, is developed with the characteristic songs of the Huichol religion. The Huichol devote much time to making very beautiful disks, yarn paintings glued with wax onto a wood backing, votive arrows, and other offerings for the gods. The Indians believe that their offerings strengthen the gods, whose existence depends on such tributes and sacrifices, and that in return the gods will protect them.

The Huichol religion puts great emphasis on the yearly peyote pilgrimage and ceremonies, which are intimately related to the growth of maize. Peyote, a small cactus whose buttons produce hallucinations, grows wild near the state of San Luis Potosí. Those who take part in the forty-day pilgrimage to collect it become priests for the duration of the march. The night before the pilgrimage begins, a dozen Indians bathe and sleep with their women in the temple. The next day many prayers are said and, carrying tobacco pouches and wearing hats decorated with feathers and squirrel tails, the men leave their women to begin the march. They are led by four captains. None of the marchers or their women bathe or wash except ceremonially, and they fast, forego salt, and abstain from sexual intercourse. When the men return, the appearance of the sacred plants in the Huichol village is celebrated; the people decorate

In the Huichol village, the cycle of human life is ordered about the religious ritual. A family prepares votive offerings for the gods. The older man wears the daily dress with a woven shoulder bag. The woman wears the *quechquemitl* with an embroidered fringe. The young man wears sashes, one over the other, with pockets hanging from the beautifully decorated fringe.

The Huichol people display an extraordinary originality in inventing objects whose purpose is to assure communication with the gods. They are innate craftsmen, and have extraordinary imagination in design. Traditional beliefs have become fused with Christianity; for example, the Morning Star, long in the Huichol pantheon, has become identified with the image of Christ. To conceive of a spiritual power in a natural form is a characteristic of the Indian mind.

Votive offerings lie here before a cross. They include arrows and other miniature objects attached to the offerings. The most beautiful of these are the feathers, sacred to the deity concerned. An arrow dedicated to the god of fire is decorated with an eagle or a parrot feather. There are also votive vessels and candles, symbols of the same god and emblems of life.

Most Indian ceremonies in Mexico have been modified by the influence of the Catholic church, but the more characteristic retain their native character. Among them is the ceremony of animal sacrifice. It was a widespread belief among pre-Columbian peoples that the maintenance and continuity of life and civilization could only be guaranteed through sacrifice—human as well as animal. The sacrificial rite was accompanied by pageantry, dance and song. It was performed not only on the great feast days of the religious calendar, but also on occasions when the aid of the gods was especially desirable: weddings, births, sickness and military or religious expeditions. The survival of this custom is clearly seen here, as Huichol men and women prepare a sacrificial animal. The blood is *agua viva* (living water), the sacred liquid offered as a drink to the gods. Taking the liquid, the gods accept the petitions of the worshippers. The petitions are presented in votive gourds ornamented with beads attached with wax. This ceremony is performed outdoors, so that Father Sun may watch.

One of the most notable contributions of the National Museum of Anthropology to the knowledge of Mexico is the series of exhibits of past and present day dwellings, common to the various regions of the country. These were built by natives, following their traditional designs and the materials to which they were accustomed. Here, a Huichol oratory, the house for the gods, has an opening over the door so that the gods can see out. To the left is the seat of the gods, forbidden to human use. If the wind blows and rustles the leaves of the tree shading the roof, the gods are pleased and will share in the offerings.

their faces with a yellow pigment obtained in the land of peyote. The festival lasts two or three days, and various ceremonies are held, including ritual bathing and the taking of peyote. The drug causes those who eat or drink it to see horrible or amusing visions; the inebriation lasts two or three days. Each man must participate once in his lifetime in the peyote pilgrimage. During the trip and for many weeks after it, he becomes a bearer of magic forces that are translated into rain, health, good harvests, and long life.

Huichol Indians yearly participate in a ceremony with peyote, one of several hallucinogenic plants used by Mexican indigenous peoples. Each year, Huichol men make a forty-day pilgrimage to bring peyote, or *jiculi*, back to their villages for the festival. A Huichol man must go to peyote country once in his lifetime, and for several weeks after the rites he is considered to be endowed with magical forces. Each expedition consists of ten to twelve men. The leader assumes the role of Grandfather Fire, and is the only one allowed to kindle fire on the journey. His is a very important role, since *jiculi* is the plant from which the God of Fire drinks. He carries a cord with as many knots as there are days in the journey and has special powers.

Huichol Indians leave the Okutzare cave, where living quarters for Father Sun have been built of saplings and straw. Before the images of the deity inside, the Indians place offerings of arrows, *ojos de Dios* (eyes of God), votive plaques, decorated vessels, and other ritual objects. The principal gods are believed to have been born in these sacred caves, which are ceremonial centers and play a vital religious role. The caves are scattered throughout Huichol lands and have been chosen for their proximity to springs or rivers, which are used as fonts for baptisms and for priestly rituals. Here the Indians pass the tests and acquire the knowledge needed for admittance to the priesthood. The water of the caves is sacred, representing the god that produced it. It is stored and carried to the shrines of villages and settlements.

TARASCAN ETHNOGRAPHY

REGION. The Tarascan Indians, more properly called Purepecha, occupy the tablelands of the state of Michoacán. The region can be divided into a rough, mountainous area, which has coniferous forests and includes the greater part of the tablelands; the lake area, a zone around Lake Pátzcuaro, which includes, culturally speaking, the Zirahuen Lagoon and, geographically, Cuitzeo; and the canyon area, called the "Eleven Towns," a narrow valley traversed by a national highway devoted to agriculture. There are 58,300 Tarascans in the three regions, and their language is Pore, commonly called Tarasco, an isolated language that has not been classified within any of the American linguistic groups.

HISTORY. The Tarascan Empire arose in about 1250 A.D. on Lake Pátzcuaro. Through conquest the Tarascan extended their dominion to almost all of the present state of Michoacán and part of the states of Guanajuato, Guerrero, and Jalisco. Their principal population centers were Tzintzuntzán, Ihuatzio, and Pátzcuaro. The conquistador Nuño de Guzman forced them to submit to Spanish rule in 1530.

ECONOMY. The Tarascan economy is based on agriculture; the main crops are maize, potatoes, wheat, and beans; some attempts have been made to introduce cotton and linseed. Many agricultural lands are communal, and others, generally small individual plots, are private property. The Tarascans augment their economy with fishing, especially on Lake Pátzcuaro, where they use the famous "butterfly" net.

HANDICRAFTS AND DRESS. Tarascans can be said to have a "wood culture." From it they fashion plows, yokes for oxen, canoes and paddles, paint trays and bowls, dwellings, and even overhead troughs to transport water. The Tarascans make inlaid wood furniture, toys, musical instruments, and masks, and notable among their handicrafts is *maqueado* work, or inlaid lacquer wooden bowls. This craft mixes pre-Hispanic tradition with Chinese and European motifs introduced during the colonial period. Tarascans also manufacture a type of pottery which is undoubtedly pre-Hispanic in origin. Textiles are also rich and greatly varied. Hats, mats, and decorative and religious objects are made from hard fibers. Metal work includes the Santa Clara hammered copperwork, forged iron, and silver with characteristic designs.

RELIGION. The Tarascans preserve traditional religious elements that have been modified by contact with modern culture. Political organization is regulated by municipal authority, which in some towns coexists with the traditional authority represented by the *carguero* (steward), entrusted with the expenses of the patron saint's festival and by the elders who have already served in that capacity. Among the most intimate expressions of the Tarascans are the *pirecuas*, songs that speak of love and bucolic themes and are accompanied by guitars. The most famous ceremonies are the "Exchange of Power" and the "Day of the Dead," which are held every year. In the "Exchange of Power," the new *carguero* receives a great crown made from confection, which he breaks into pieces and distributes among his friends and relatives who, on accepting the gift, promise to help him with the costs of the festival. The "Day of the Dead" is a ceremony held annually for three years after the death of an individual; the relatives prepare dishes for the deceased, who supposedly returns to earth yearly, and decorate his tomb with flowers.

A young girl launders clothes on flat stones at the edge of Lake Pátzcuaro. For the Tarascans inhabiting its shores and the island of Jánitzo, the lake is a transportation route, a source of income from fishing and duck hunting, and a washing place.

Lake Pátzcuaro lies in Mexico's largest lake area, between the cities of Guadalajara and Mexico City, only a stone's throw from ▶ Morelia, capital of Michoacán. Pátzcuaro, today a national monument, was founded by the missionary Don Vasco de Quiroga on the site of a centuries old Tarascan village. It is built on the hills that slope back from the lake, at almost the same altitude as Mexico City. Life in Pátzcuaro combines Indian and Spanish traditions. Friday is market day when the people from the other lake-side towns and the lake's island stream in by dugout canoes to sell and buy their varied folk-products: trays, baskets, masks, pottery, blankets and copper goods. Jánitzo, located on a mountain island, is the home of the lake's most proficient fishermen. Nets line its streets, hanging from poles to which canoes are moored. With butterfly nets, the delight of painters and photographers as well as the theme of many a song and folk dance, fishermen catch the *charal*. This small, transparent, delicate white fish is a staple of the regional diet, particularly consumed throughout Lent. On the opposite page is seen a museum exhibit of the fishing industry of the Pátzcuaro region. A huge *chinchorro* (dragnet) is grace-fully draped over a small *icharutu* (canoe), carved from a tree-trunk. The *chinchorro*, which has a finely woven central section, is the most common and effective net used in the region. Below is seen a local fisherman on the lake with the *uiripo* (butterfly net), which is handled in a spoon-like fashion to catch the tiny *charal*.

Frontispiece:
Los Viejitos (The Little Old Men), a characteristic Tarascan dance, is performed during an important fiesta at Charapán, Michoacán. The "Little Old Man" wears a mask and a white wig of *ixtle*. The role of Maringuis, danced here by a woman, is often played by a man.

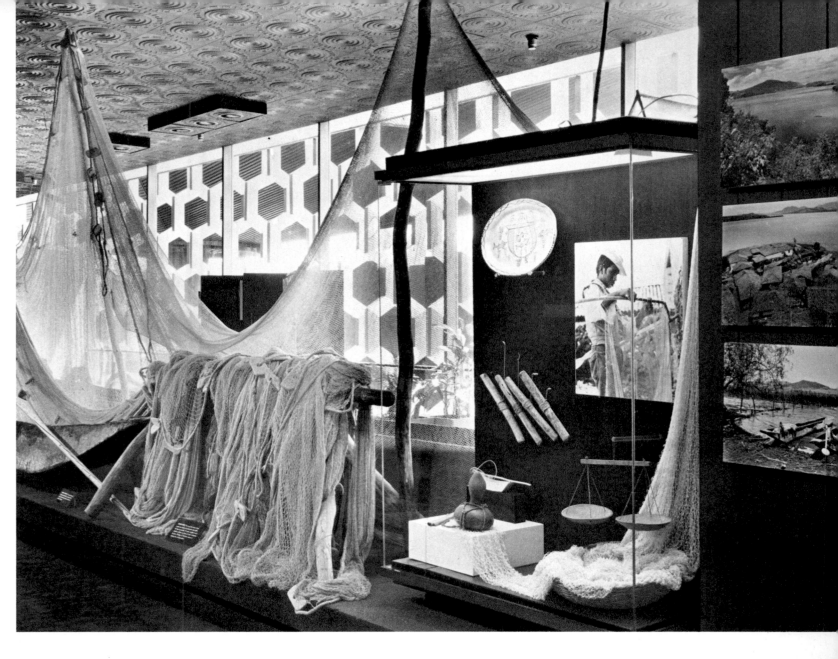

At the festival of Corpus Christi, hunters from Charapán cut up several animals they have killed, which will later be roasted and eaten. At the festival, celebrated throughout the Tarascan plateau, the villagers gather in groups in the streets according to their trades and set up for business: toy makers are outstanding. Blanket-weavers make tiny samples which they give away, and women go about with great baskets filled with *tortillas*.

◄ The museum displays a typical Tarascan Indian house with columns carved in baroque style. This traditional mountain dwelling is called *troje* (granary), probably because corn is stored in the attic. The walls and floor are built of boards supported by huge beams; the roof is generally tiled and has four inclined surfaces.

◄ Since colonial times, the village of Santa Clara del Cobre, Michoacán, has specialized in the production of hammered copper articles ranging from little candle-holders, ashtrays, dishes, and pitchers to enormous pans used throughout Mexico for frying *carnitas* and pork cracklings. The copper, formerly local, is now from Mexico City.

A Michoacán Indian uses a spindle to wind thread. Since pre-Hispanic times the Indians of Mexico have used the *malacate*, in which a stick is passed through a small cylindrical section, usually made of clay. In the original spindle, simpler than the one shown here, the point of the stick was rested on a squash and the instrument spun to wind cotton or *ixtle* thread onto it.

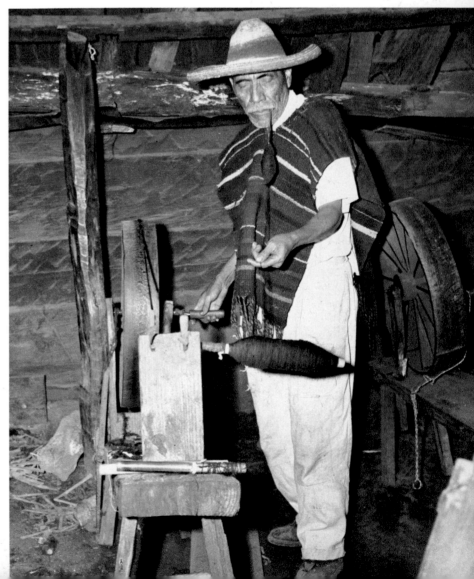

OTOMI-PAME ETHNOGRAPHY

REGION. The Otomi groups live about 60 miles northwest of Mexico City, in the areas of Toluca, Ixtlahuaca, and Atlacomulco, in the State of Mexico. The region consists of a series of small valleys with an average altitude of 6,500 to 10,000 feet above sea level. The climate is temperate and rainy, and the area is characterized by abundant vegetation of zacaton and spiny chaparral. The Otomi also occupy the Mezquital Valley, an extensive and arid plain some 100 miles north of Mexico City; the valley has limited natural resources. Few parts of the region are cultivated, due to the extreme shortage of water, which must be raised from deep wells, but the maguey grows abundantly.

POPULATION. Some 80,000 Otomi Indians live in the Mezquital Valley. In Toluca, Ixtlahuaca, and Atlacomulco are another 200,000. In the states of Querétaro, San Luis Potosí, and Guanajuato are other Otomi Indians, who are difficult to identify because of the influence of neighboring Nahua groups; they are the Pame-Chichimec Indians, who number some 2,800 persons.

LANGUAGE. The Otopame linguistic family includes four different tongues, all of which are spoken by the Otomi groups: Pame, Chichimec Jonaz, Otomi-Mazahua, and Matlatzinc, which includes Ocuiltec.

HISTORY. The Otomi captured the Mezquital Valley, the Basin of Mexico, and adjacent regions where the Teotihuacán culture had flourished, between the years 650 and 900 A.D. Their culture attained different levels; the Matlatzinc and the Otomi-Mazahua, for example, possessed a culture similar to that of Mesoamerica, although the Otomi-Mazahua had some cultural traits characteristic of the north. Their economy was based principally on agriculture. They possessed a religious organization and constructed civil ceremonial centers. The Otomi Indians who settled in the Mezquital Valley and Querétaro had a culture similar to that of northern Mesoamerica, although some of their traits and customs centered on the exploitation of the maguey plant, as they still do today. This plant was also utilized by other Indian groups. The Otomi Indians of today are practically isolated from the rest of Mexico, and the programs of social integration promoted by revolutionary governments have failed. They still continue to be somewhat nomadic, and do not integrate well even with other Indian groups.

ECONOMY. The Matlatzinc-Ocuiltec and the Otomi-Mazahua Indians are most concerned with agriculture. The Otomi-Mazahua plant maize, beans, squash, wheat, barley, and lima beans. They also catch fish which they eat or sell in the marketplace. Thus, their economy is more prosperous than that of the Otomi of the Mezquital Valley and the state of Querétaro, who are wild-plant gatherers and who preserve a good part of their pre-Hispanic origin and continue to support themselves by the exploitation of the maguey plant. However, the maguey is not cultivated with wisdom and little care is given it. Pulque and maguey worms are obtained from it; the most tender leaves are given to cattle as fodder, and the others are left to dry and are then scraped to obtain the *ixtle* fibers with which various objects are woven. The maguey also has medical properties and is used to construct walls or roofs of houses.

◄ The dance of *Los Concheros* (The Shell Men) is one of the most colorful in Mexico. Named for the guitars used, which are made from the shell of the armadillo, it is performed by many groups, some of the best being the Otomi. As many as fifty colorfully dressed *concheros* make up what is called a *mesa*, or group. Sometimes the guitars are encrusted with sea shells and they are considered to be works of art.

The maguey plant grows abundantly in the very arid Mezquital Valley, and is the center of the Otomi Indian life. Its sap gives nourishment, medicine, and pulque, a beverage that substitutes for water in this dry region. Its firm leaves provide building material and fuel. Before the Conquest, paper, needles, and fiber for nets, blankets and clothing were made from the maguey.

The Pame-Chichimec Indians are a marginal group and base their economy on rudimentary agriculture, handicrafts, and breeding of small animals. Although they do not form such a homogeneous cultural group as the previously mentioned groups, they have certain common cultural characteristics.

HANDICRAFTS. The Otomi Indians augment their economy with various handicrafts, such as their elaborate basketwork. A rough pottery is also produced, in forms reminiscent of pre-Hispanic ceramics. Cotton, wool, and *ixtle* cloth are produced, and blouses, purses, sashes, and *quechquemitls* are embroidered. The Otomi-Mazahua also work in silver, and their embroidery is very ornate.

DWELLING. Otomi housing ranges from scattered huts of maguey leaves, organ cactus and mud, which are united by a common church and water hole, to Otomi-Mazahua towns concentrated around a school,

The extremely deep wells of the Mezquital Valley are operated by groups of women who push the primitive mechanism with which they pull up their filled buckets. The parched, harsh valley has no springs, pools, or streams, and the people dig communal wells to obtain water for their animals, their crops, and themselves.

The role of wood in the Tarascan economy, or of cotton and wool among the Zapotecs, is played by the maguey among the Otomi. With strong, skillful hands an Otomi rolls dried maguey fiber for braiding into bags, nets, ropes, and other articles. The multiple use of one resource is a lesson the Indian has learned well from poverty.

The Otomi groups are found in many different and disparate zones of Mexico. This geographic dislocation reflects their fate. Ever since the Toltecs expelled them from the central highlands, they have struggled to find a permanent home and settlement. For a long time, the Otomi were felt to be indifferent, distrustful and shrewd. Their name has been used in a pejorative way since the time of the Aztecs, and even today nearly all programs to integrate them, or acculturate them into the national society have failed. However, in spite of poverty, dispersion and the un-hospitable landscape which they must often inhabit, the Otomi Indian is a patient and skillful craftsman, and makes lovely handicrafts with whatever materials he has available. He joins reeds and palm leaves with cane threads to make imaginat-ively designed bird cages, painted baskets, and hats *(left)*. In the photographs, an old woman carries baskets on her back, and a man tries on hats in the market place.

Pottery reflects the bareness of Otomi life in the Mezquital Valley. The vessels are simply shaped and only occasionally decor-ated with timid designs. This gives them a particularly austere and noble quality that contrasts with the more decorative pottery of other states such as Michoacán and Oaxaca, where pottery is colorful and displays complicated techniques and glazes.

In a museum exhibit, Otomi of the Mezquital Valley, wearing traditional dress, weave and make baskets and pottery. The boy holds a *coa*, a primitive planting stick. The woman seated on the left is preparing to weave, using the waist loom in front of her. The woman standing in the center spins thread from fiber, using an ancient *malacate*. In the photographs are shown the processing and end-products of the maguey. After eight or nine months of growth, the plant is ripe. Its core is pierced by a *chiquero*, who draws out the juice by sucking on a long, thin, straw-like gourd. After fermentation, the juice becomes pulque, one of Mexico's most typical and inexpensive drinks. The man in the foreground of the exhibit stretches the skin of an animal he has hunted for food. All these varied activities are evidence of the resourcefulness of the Indian villagers.

church, and municipal hall. The quadrangular houses in the towns are made of adobe and brick faced with mortar, and have tiled roofs; they are located in the center of a patio, at one end of which is a chapel with a domestic altar. The shrine is also quadrangular, has no windows, and has a single door; within is an altar dedicated to the favorite saint of the family, crosses, censers, and the like.

RELIGION. Religious festivals honor the town's patron saint and are organized around the church. Dances such as "Moors and Christians" are performed, accompanied by drums, flutes, whistles, and rattles. The dancers carry standards and sometimes the Mexican flag. One of the most famous dances is *Los Concheros* which, with *La Malinche*, forms an important part of the Pame-Chichimec religious festivals. These dances, however, by no means originated with these groups, and they are danced throughout Mexico.

ETHNOGRAPHY OF THE SIERRA DE PUEBLA

REGION. Some 160,000 members of indigenous groups inhabit about 4,000 square miles, along a strip of the eastern Sierra Madre from the central plateau to the Gulf lowland. The area is bounded on the north by Ixhuatlán, Veracruz, and on the south from Tulancingo, Hidalgo, to Zacapoaxtla, Puebla. The Sierra de Puebla, a region of deep canyons, is the point of contact between the highlands and the coast, in a geographical as well as a cultural sense.

POPULATION. The eastern part of the Sierra de Puebla is inhabited by 50,000 Totonac Indians who are in contact with the coast where the rest of their group lives. In the northwestern area live some 5,000 Tepehua Indians, and in the western and southern part 28,000 Otomi Indians and 75,000 Nahuas.

LANGUAGE. The languages spoken in the region belong to the Totonac, Uto-Aztec, and Otopame families and take the names of the Indians speaking them.

HISTORY. The Sierra de Puebla as a cultural area is of great interest; since the classical Mesoamerican epoch, it has succeeded in integrating diverse ethnic groups from different states—Nahua, Otomi, Totonac, and Tepehua—ignoring ecological, linguistic, and political barriers. The zone is a huge "region of refuge" in which ancient traits such as certain handicrafts, dances and shamanistic practices gradually lost by neighboring groups have been preserved.

ECONOMY. Very many members of indigenous groups live in settlements devoted to agriculture. Abundant rainfall and mists make the land very fertile, and two maize crops are generally harvested each year. Coffee-growing is becoming increasingly important, as is the cultivation of sugar cane and peanuts. There is little hunting or fishing, although among the Otomi of San Pablito different fishing methods are used, ranging from poisons obtained from the verbascum plant to dynamite.

HANDICRAFTS AND DRESS. Since pre-Hispanic times the Otomi and Totonac women have been famous for their weaving. Presently the most notable article of clothing of the Sierra de Puebla is the *quechquemitl*; its design varies, and the wearer's town can be identified by its weave. The most common color for skirts is white, although some Nahua women wear dark wool. The Xalacapán sashes made on backstrap looms are famous, as are those of Nauhzontla, which have many designs embroidered with silk thread. Male attire is simpler and consists of a coarse, white cotton shirt and trousers with a dark *serape*. An exception is the beaded shirt worn by the Otomi Indian on his wedding day. In San Pablito, pre-Hispanic techniques of manufacturing paper from the barks of the *amate*, nettle, and blackberry bushes are still used, and the paper is made into dolls for magical purposes.

◄ The face of a Nahua woman from Cuetzalán, Puebla, reflects the loss of the gaiety and amiability characteristic of the region. She has abandoned her beautiful Indian dress for the shawl of the mestizos. The state of Puebla was the setting of many quite recent revolutions.

A woman wears a costume almost identical to that of her pre-Hispanic ancestors. The enormous headdress of green and purple wool cords is braided into her hair. A finely woven *quechquemitl* is then tucked into the headdress.

The deputy mayor of San Andres Zicuilán, a Nahua village, is dressed in a traditional muslin shirt, white pants, black wool *serape*, and hat. His office and institution are greatly respected.

DWELLING. The typical Otomi dwelling is a quadrangular house with a straw or palm-leaf roof, with walls of cane, planking, or wattle. Adjacent to the house is a *temazcal*, a kind of sauna bath common to the region; it is made of stone and mud and has a flat roof, although the Tepehua Indians of Huehuetla prefer a circular shape. Vapor is obtained by throwing water on red-hot stones, and ritual baths are carried out inside. The Otomi Indians do not consider this structure important, and in Cuetzalán and among some Tepehuas it is reduced to a framework of sticks which is covered when used. Some dwellings also contain individual shrines like those of the Otomi in San Pablito, or communal shrines like those of the Tepehua Indians.

RELIGION. Some ceremonies and beliefs of pre-Hispanic origin have been preserved in the Sierra de Puebla. Outstanding are the dance-games such as *El Volador* (The Birdman), and *Los Quetzalines* (The Dance of the Quetzal Bird); and pure dances like the *Acatlaxquis*, *Santiagueros*, and *Tambulán*. Shamanistic

◄ On Sunday a market is set up in the principal square and surrounding streets of San Francisco Cuetzalán, one of the most picturesque villages of the Sierra de Puebla. The Indians, dressed in their best clothes, come to buy and sell their products. To this day, the market and the particular day chosen for it, continue to be the heart of Indian life. It is here that the Indian exhibits his creativeness in the articles he buys and sells, chats with friends, and finds release in fiestas. Nahua and Totonac languages are spoken in this typical mestizo village.

Many Otomi inhabit the western and southern zones of the Sierra de Puebla. The Otomi Indians of San Pablito employ a special method of collective fishing for river trout in the spring. By crushing the leaves of the *lechuguilla* or *barbasco* plant, they obtain saponin, which they throw into the water to stun the fish. Then, moving downstream in a line (*above right*), they catch them in sacks (*below*). They also use poisons and dynamite. In the belief that fish have a keen sense of smell and find the scent of Christians offensive, the first successful fisherman (*above left*) bites off a piece of the tail and swallows it, thereby destroying his smell.

Figures made by Otomi and Tepehua Indians of the Sierra de Puebla symbolize human and supernatural beings. These figures, made from *amate*, a bark paper, are used in many religious ceremonies. Dark figures are used for incantations and represent bad spirits, and the whitish ones represent good spirits. Tissue paper is used to make the dolls which represent various plants, with representative colors: purple for beans, green for bananas and so on. The figure on the far left represents vegetables, probably tomatoes, and the next two appear to be representations of the devil. The small figure in pyramidal form is related to the "Lord of the Animals." The other three are also associated with fruits and vegetables, the one on the far right probably with chili pepper.

An Otomi woman of San Pablito wears the beautiful *quechquemitl*, with its curved magenta stripe, which is typical of her village. This garment varies enormously among the different groups in the Sierra de Puebla. For example, the *quechquemitl* of Cuetzalán and Atla is made of very fine, embroidered white chiffon, whereas that of Huehuetla is so thickly embroidered with colored yarns that it looks like felt. The Otomi Indians of San Pablito and Santa Ana use a special technique, the curved sash weave, executed on backstrap looms.

She is making *amate* (bark paper) by the traditional pre-Hispanic technique. She soaks the fibers in a deep wooden tray, lays out the shape of fibers on a board, fills it in, and beats it with a flat stone until she obtains a sheet that is almost transparent. Behind her, on boards, are finished sheets set out to dry in the hot sun.

No recorded pre-Hispanic music survived the Conquest, largely because it was intimately connected with the Indian religions which the Spaniards rigorously suppressed. Nonetheless, Indian music and dance heard and seen in the country are still haunted by the ancient musical traditions. Significantly, contemporary scholars, musicians and dancers have turned to its study, preservation and recreation, as one more aspect of Mexico's quest for its own past. A museum exhibit includes handicrafts, clothing and photographs of ceremonies of the Totonac, Nahua, Otomi and Tepehua Indians of the Sierra de Puebla. Displays include little Indian drums from the Otomi village of San Pablito, rattles and a *teponaxtle*, a pre-Hispanic type of drum made from a hollow tree trunk and played with two rubber-tipped sticks *(lower right)*. Photographs show the dance of the *Acatlaxquis* (those who have sugar cane), which is accompanied by drum and flute, with a rattle which sets the rhythm. Canes with feathers are also used. The serpent between the two figures is another pre-Hispanic device used in certain dances.

practices, popular in origin, still survive; they are linked to the daily life of the indigenous farmer and are practiced by medicine men or *adivinos* (soothsayers). Among the Otomi and Tepehua Indians, the medicine men and soothsayers direct a large number of ceremonies, called "customs," which are acts of propitiation to the ancient deities and are linked with the agricultural cycle. One custom invokes the goddess of the lagoon if the rains have failed to arrive on time; others are linked with the life cycle and with rituals surrounding birth, puberty, healing, witchcraft, and death. The Tepehua medicine man has his own chapel with an altar, where he guards a pre-Hispanic idol and a crystal ball to "see" and predict. In these ceremonies paper dolls made from *amate* are used. The dark ones are used for incantations and to represent bad spirits, and the whitish ones represent good spirits. Tissue paper is used to make the dolls that represent the various plants, with representative colors: purple for beans, green for bananas, and so forth.

Splendid Indian dances, called *Quetzales*, are performed in the villages to the south of Veracruz and in the mountain areas of Puebla and Hidalgo. They are inspired by the *quetzal*, the magnificent bird that lives in the highlands of southern Mexico and Central America, and was much prized by the pre-Columbian peoples because of the brilliance of its plumage. The dancers' costumes have bright colors, and red generally predominates. Their shirts, white or colored, are decorated with ribbons. They wear large, silk handkerchiefs, long trousers and a cape decorated with fringes, sequins and small mirrors. But the most stunning part of their dress is the large headdress *(above)*. It is like a huge wheel, which can be as much as twelve feet in diameter, made of colored cardboard and decorated with feathers. The wheel is attached to a cone-shaped hat. Because of the width of these brims, the dance itself is stately and simple. *(Below) Los Negritos* is a dance performed by the Nahua and Totonac Indians of the Sierra de Puebla. One dancer is dressed as La Malinche, the Indian woman who guided Cortes through Mexico. Some are dressed as clowns and others wear masks.

ETHNOGRAPHY OF OAXACA

REGION. The indigenous languages and cultures of Oaxaca are unusually heterogeneous. They fall into three regions: the Mixtec and Zapotec area and northern Oaxaca. The Mixtec area, in the west, extends northward into Puebla and westward into Guerrero. The Zapotec area, including the central valleys of Oaxaca, the mountainous region of Ixtlán and Juárez, extends to Chiapas in the northwest, to the Pacific Ocean in the south, and beyond the isthmus of Tehuantepec in the east. The northern zone of Oaxaca extends along the peaks and slopes of the Mixe and Huautla Mountains.

POPULATION. The Indian population of Oaxaca is the largest in the nation, nearly twenty-five percent of the total. In the Mixtec area live nearly 200,000 Mixtec, 7,000 Trique, 5,000 Chocho, 2,000 Amuzgo, 1,000 Ixcatec, and 1,000 Nahua Indians. In the Zapotec area, some 270,000 Zapotecs live in the central valleys, sharing the southern part with some 13,000 Chatin and 6,500 Chontal Indians. The northern zone is inhabited by more than 200,000 Mazatec, Chinantec, Mixe, Cuicatec and Mixtec Indians. In the jungle zone of the isthmus, live a group of Zoque Indians and some 3,000 Huave or Mareño.

LANGUAGE. The native tongues of Oaxaca and the linguistic families to which they belong are complex. The Mixeño group includes the Mixe and Zoque tongues. The Comecrudeño includes the Oaxaca Chontal, one of the oldest languages in the country. Huave is an isolated tongue, while Mixtequeño includes Mixtec, Cuicatec, Amuzgo and Trique. Both the Chatin and Zapotec are linguistic families, the latter with many local variants. There are many other dialects in the state.

ECONOMY. The economy of the Mixtec region is based on maize cultivation, often augmented by crops of beans, wheat, coffee, and sugar cane, and the weaving of palm-leaf hats, sold outside the region. In the fertile central valleys the Zapotecs cultivate maize, wheat, castor-oil plants, fruits and vegetables. Besides being the most prosperous of the state's Indian groups, the Zapotecs have become integrated into the Western cultural patterns of the cities. In the isthmus, the basic economic activity is the cultivation of maize, as well as beans, sesame, fruit, and cocoa. But here it is the women who control the trade. There is abundant livestock and fishing in the zone. The Huave Indians, strongly influenced by the Zapotecs, sell them their marine products; the Chontal and Chatin groups cultivate the maguey plant, the source of *mezcal*. The Mazatecs, Cuicatecs, and Mixe cultivate maize for national consumption. Most Chinantecs and some Mazatecs produce tobacco on the banks of the tributaries of the Papaloapan, and their fertile lands enable them to harvest two maize crops a year.

HANDICRAFTS AND DRESS. In the Mixtec region Trique women wear short wraparound skirts and long profusely decorated *huipiles*. In Pinotepa the Mixtec women go bare-breasted and wear skirts of alternating cotton and silk strips dyed blue, brown, and red. The women from the coastal regions also use *hui-*

◄ A Mixtec woman buys a net at the market in Pinotepa de San Luis, in the Mixteca region of Oaxaca. She wears a *huipil* over her head and shoulders. Her breasts will be covered only twice in her life, when she marries and when she dies.

In the torrid valleys and jungles, and along the Pacific coast, the Mixtec house is round with a conical grass roof built on a framework of sticks joined with mud. The pot at the top of the cone sheds rain water. This style of dwelling shows the influence of African slaves brought to Mexico by the Spanish. It was equally well suited for the damp jungle climate of Mexico.

In the warm coastal climate, Mixtec women wear only a wrap-around skirt while at work in their villages. Here they grind corn for *tortillas*, in the pre-Hispanic manner. The kitchen is built outdoors and is thatched with palm leaves. Kitchen utensils are stored under the roof. From the number working, it appears that they are grinding corn for a fiesta, the traditional way a village has of renewing its group identity. Despite its pagan color and drama, the fiesta has ritual importance because it always involves a local cult.

piles, but in the lowlands women wear Western-style clothing. Masculine attire is less varied and consists mainly of sandals *(huaraches)*, coarse cotton trousers and shirts, except on the coast where traditional clothing is worn. The Zapotecs of the valleys engage in traditional textile and basket weaving; outstanding pottery is made in Coyotepec and Atzampa. Among the Zapotecs of the mountains, the elegant costumes of Yalaltec women are outstanding with their silk embroidery complemented by a headdress *(tlacoyal)* of twisted black yarn. The Mixe and Huautla zones are especially interesting for the great variety and quantity of native dress worn by the women.

Dwelling. In the Mixtec region houses are made of saplings with thatched roofs, often circular in form, with conical roofs showing African influence. In wooded areas the houses are quadrangular with log walls and shingled roofs. In the dry regions construction is of limestone or adobe, with palm-leaf or thatched roofs, and the *temazcal* (a sauna-like bath) is more frequent here than in other areas. In Chinantla and the tropical zone the proportions of the houses attract attention, for they generally have only one room with sapling walls and high roofs of red thatch.

Religion. The valley Zapotecs, because of their proximity to the capital, are Roman Catholic. The activities of Indian life show a profound religious sentiment mixing ancient and Catholic elements. This sentiment is directed by the leaders or *mandones*, who still guide much of community life. It is present in forms of nature worship and enjoyment. The Mixe, for example, offer animal blood to the earth goddess, and in their mountain caves worship the "rain, thunder and mountain lords." The sea figures prominently in Huave dances and ceremonies. The outstanding Zapotec Feather Dance on the Conquest of Mexico, though more nearly secular, still reflects Indian piety.

Trique girls of Copala, Oaxaca, show off their *huipiles* during school recess. The school is in the background.

Seen here is a wonderful variety of garments worn in the various parts of Oaxaca. They are remarkable not only for their variety of color, but also for the different styles which often identify inhabitants of certain villages.

Mixtec women from the coastal regions, wearing multicolored *huipiles* and *pozahuancos*, obtain goods at the regional fairs. The gourds which they carry on their heads are used for drinking water, food, or fragile objects.

Above left :

A Huave woman still wears the traditional wrap-around skirt. Her outer *huipil* is borrowed from her Zapotec neighbors of Tehuantepec and Juchitán, Oaxaca.

Above right :

A Mazatec woman wears a *huipil* beautifully embroidered with designs of birds and flowers, and carries objects in a net on her head. The Mazatecs' wrap-around skirts are almost always red or blue with narrow white stripes.

The Tacuate Indians are one of the few groups of the Mixtec region whose men still wear the traditional costume, outstanding for its design and fine embroidery.

The Chinantec Indian of the Chinantla region in Oaxaca uses the various instruments exhibited in the museum for fishing (nets, a raft and a basket).

A Zapotec Indian of Ayutla, one of the more fertile areas in the state of Oaxaca, uses the wooden plow, rather than the traditional *coa* or digging stick, for cultivating the steep, very fertile hillsides where maize, beans, sesame, fruit and cocoa are grown.

A Zapotec dwelling has a yard, the function of which is similar to that of the patio in the Spanish colonial home: it is the setting for much of family life. In the front is a corn crib on wheels, and in the rear a kiln for firing pottery.

A Mixe woman rolls corn on a *metate* until it becomes dough for making *tortillas*, a staple in the diet of Meso-american Indians since the beginning of their cultures. The dough will be shaped into a ball and then patted into perfectly flat cakes by skillful hands.

221

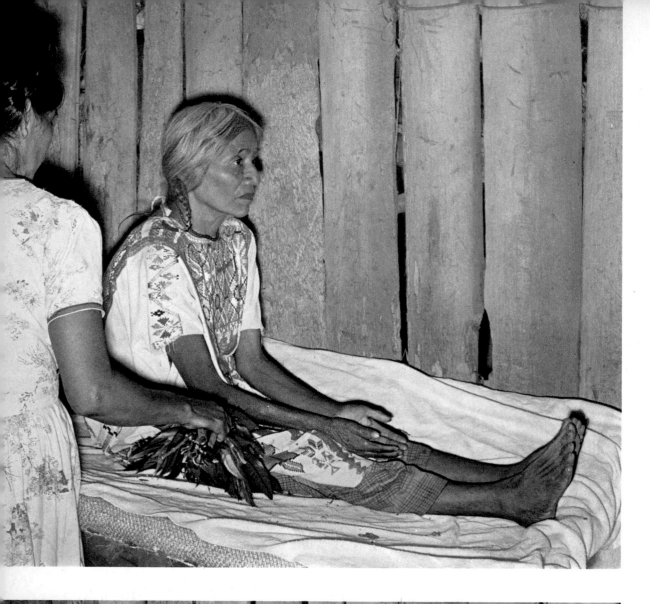

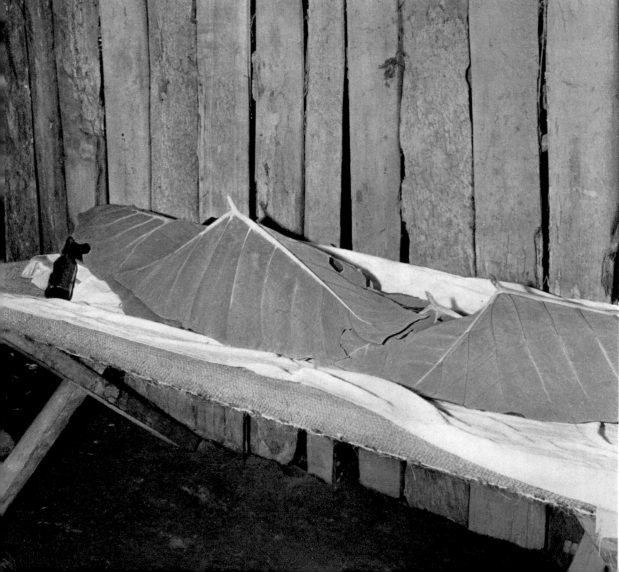

In Chiltepec, Oaxaca, a Chinantec town, methods of curing sickness, and such ailments as "loss of soul" and "frights" are still magical. After diagnosing the illness, the medicine man (or woman, as here) puts the patient on a cot (*above left*) and "cleanses" her with a handful of medicinal leaves, passing them over her body several times. Later, while drinking *aguardiente*, an alcoholic drink made from sugar cane, and chanting invocations and prayers to the spirits, she covers the sick person's body with plantain leaves (*below left*).

Another treatment uses witchcraft. A woman witch doctor "smokes" the patient and invokes the powers of pagan and Christian gods; then she sucks out the evil from the patient's head (*opposite*) and cleanses the body by passing an egg or a black hen over it.

ETHNOGRAPHY OF THE GULF COAST OF MEXICO

REGION. The central and northern area of the geographical zone known as the Gulf of Mexico, including parts of the states of San Luis Potosí, Veracruz, Hidalgo, and Tamaulipas, is inhabited by groups of Totonac, Huastec, and Nahua Indians. The Totonacs occupy mainly the central area between the mouth of the Antigua River to the Cazones River, called Totonacapán. Large groups of Totonac Indians inhabit the Sierra de Puebla, but only those living in the coastal lowlands are discussed here. The indigenous Nahua tribes living in the coastal lowlands are found in the Huastec region, an area that also includes part of the previously mentioned four states. Here too are found the Huastec Indians and small groups of Otomi and Tepehua Indians. The main centers of Nahua population are Huejutla, in the state of Hidalgo, and Chicontepec, in Veracruz, although the Nahua population also extends along the coast. The most important Huastec groups are found at Tancahuitz, Aquismon, Landajas, Cuidad Valles, Tampamolon in San Luis Potosí, and the zone between the Panuco River to Tuxpán in Veracruz.

POPULATION. According to the 1960 census, 29,911 Totonac and 67,238 monolingual Nahua Indians live in Veracruz. Those speaking the Huastec tongue number about 60,000.

LANGUAGE. Totonac forms a linguistic family that includes both Totonac and Tepehua; Nahua belongs to the Uto-Azteca family of languages; and the Huastec tongue is part of the Mayan family.

HISTORY. At Totonacapán, the Spaniards found two important population centers, Tajín and Cempoala. Their inhabitants belonged to the great Mesoamerican civilizations and had created a culture which, although greatly influenced by the classic Teotihuacán period, was distinctively their own. They traded widely, and their principal crops were maize and cotton. The Nahuas arrived in the region before the Spanish Conquest, colonized various places, and expanded their dominion to other towns, which were forced to pay them tribute. Invasions made by the Chichimecs perhaps left some vestiges of their culture in the area. The Huastecs had occupied the region from an epoch perhaps earlier than the Christian era, establishing themselves throughout the central and southern Veracruz area and in Tabasco.

ECONOMY. The economy of the Gulf Coast peoples is based principally on agriculture. Such fruit trees as avocado, *zapote* (sapodilla), lemon, and orange are cultivated, as well as maize, beans, squash, chili pepper, and sweet potatoes. The main crops in the Totonac zone are sugar cane and vanilla.

HANDICRAFTS AND DRESS. The Totonac women, in addition to helping with the agricultural tasks, are entrusted with spinning and weaving cotton, which by tradition is one of their duties. Although influenced by Western styles, their dress is very colorful. The men wear coarse white trousers, tied at the ankles,

A Veracruz woman's physical characteristics identify her as an Indian, but her clothing, and that of her children, is mestizo. The state of Veracruz has a variety of human types, since peoples of Spanish blood, Negroes, and the many indigenous types have intermingled.

A traditional Totonac house is reproduced in the museum. Shared by all the family, the house serves for every activity, and when money is available, additional rooms are built. The whole village helps to build a house for a newly married couple; until then, the newlyweds live in the house of the bride's father, and the bridegroom reciprocates by helping him in the fields.

The Huastec family of Señor Martín Hernández sits outside their house in Silozúchil, in Tantoyuca, Veracruz. The dwelling is a simple mudcovered framework of poles and cane with a palm-leaf roof, cool in the warm weather, yet resistant to rains.

Negroid features are not uncommon among the Indians and Mestizos of Veracruz, for the Spaniards brought African slaves to the area of the country. This young man wears a *charro* hat.

The cultivation of vanilla in Papantla and in Tajín is extremely remunerative, and permits the women to dress with a certain degree of luxury.

boots, palm-leaf hats, and bags which hang from the shoulder. The Nahua Indians of the region manufacture ceramics. This is a task of the women, and the principal production center is Chililico in the municipality of Huejutla. Nahua women also produce magnificent textiles on backstrap looms. The main handicrafts of the Huastec Indians are *morrales* or bags made from the regional maguey, and feminine apparel which is amongst the most beautiful in Mexico. They make a *quechquemitl* embroidered with colorful yarns depicting animals, plants, and flowers in beautiful and varied designs.

DWELLING. Houses are generally rectangular, but sometimes square. The walls are of cane, wood planking, or both; the roof is built on vertical pilings which support horizontal beams, on top of which rest palm leaves or tiles. Domestic altars decorated with hand-woven, circular objects of palm leaf are frequently found inside Totonac houses. The altars are covered with cloths on which the images of saints appear, and offerings are placed around them. Near the house is a *temazcal* made of stone, mud, and small logs. Frequently a trellis is built over the *temazcal* to protect it from rain. Also ovens, stills, and primitive fruit presses are built to obtain juice from sugar cane.

RELIGION. The religious syncretism that mixes pre-Hispanic and Christian traditions predominates among the Totonac, Nahua, and Huastec Indians of the Gulf Coast. Thus, the main religious festival is that of the patron saint of the village, and many dances, like "Moors and Christians", *Santiagueros*, *Los Negritos*, *Huahuas*, and the famous *El Volador* (The Birdman) are performed at the fair on Corpus Christi Day.

The Totonac Indians have a complete system of magic medicine, and they believe that illness and death can be caused by a "fright," the "evil eye," or malignant spirits. The Huastec Indians, mainly those of San Luis Potosí, who are more conservative, have medicine men who devote their time to curing the sick by applying their knowledge of traditional medicine, based on curative herbs and plants.

El Volador (The Birdman) is one of the most spectacular dances of Mexico. It is perhaps the one most authentically preserved from pre-Hispanic times, although the costumes now reflect a European influence.

Five men are chosen to perform the dance. In the past, the dancers dressed as eagles or other birds. One is the captain, and four take the roles of birdmen. A tall, strong, straight tree is stripped of its branches and bark and set upright in the main square of the town. A wooden cylinder is attached to the top of the trunk, with a frame from which hang the four ropes to which the birdmen are tied. The captain (*above left*) stands on top of the cylinder, playing a drum and flute, and dances, turning to the four corners of the universe. Then the four birdmen, tied by their ankles and hanging head down, slowly descend (*below left and opposite*). The number of circles they turn before touching the earth varies, but in pre-Hispanic times, and even now on certain occasions, they circled thirteen times. The number of turns multiplied by the four birdmen equals the number of years of the pre-Hispanic calendar: fifty-two, divided into four, thirteen-year periods. *El Volador* undoubtedly has an intimate relation to worship of the sun. The captain who turns toward the cardinal points and the birdmen dressed as eagles (birds of the sun), make this clear. The descending eagle represents the setting of the sun at dusk, and has the same name as a great Mexican hero, Cuauhtemoc (Eagle That Falls), the last Aztec emperor.

The Gulf Coast Indians also perform other dances of great interest. The *Comanche*, a very ancient dance and possibly a heritage received by the Nahuas from the Chichimec groups that invaded the zone in pre-Hispanic times, is performed by a single person who adorns his head with feathers, paints his body red, and carries a bow and arrow, the symbols of the hunter.

MAYAN ETHNOGRAPHY

REGION. The Mayan groups inhabit the lowlands and the highlands of the states of Tabasco, Chiapas, Campeche, and Yucatán, and the Territory of Quintana Roo: these groups also extend down to British Honduras, Guatemala, and the western regions of Honduras and El Salvador. Except for the highland regions of Chiapas, the territory they occupy is predominantly warm in climate. In the lowlands the soil is calcareous, and the region is humid and cut through by rivers. The highland regions are cold in climate and have coniferous forests.

POPULATION. The Mayan groups of Chiapas are the Chol, Maya, Tzeltal, Tzotzil, Mame and Tojolabal, and some Quiche and Lacandon. These groups total approximately 382,000 people. In the Yucatán Peninsula live a total of about 357,000 Indians properly called Maya: about 36,400 in Campeche, 296,000 in Yucatán, and 24,900 in Quintana Roo. About 23,500 Chontals live in the state of Tabasco.

LANGUAGE. Although all the Mayan tongues are related, some so differ, that they do not seem to belong to the same linguistic family. From a linguistic viewpoint the Huastec Indians should be included in the Mayan family, although they inhabit an area that is far distant, geographically and culturally, from the Mayan region. The Mayan languages take the names of the indigenous groups that speak them. In the 1960 census a total of 762,361 Indians (not including the Huastecs) spoke the Mayan tongues.

HISTORY. The Mayan groups are heirs to one of the great Mesoamerican cultures. For reasons still unknown, around the tenth century A.D., the Maya abandoned the great cities of Tikal, Copan, Palenque and Bonampak, where they had settled and brought their flourishing culture to a stage of classical perfection. They sought other places in which to settle and began to come under the influence of the Nahuatls, as the ruins of Chichén Itzá show. The Nahuatl influence caused modifications of certain aspects of their religion and increased human sacrifice and war. Various alliances were established between the Mayan and Nahuatl peoples. Their last alliance, the product of an especially bloody war, marked the full decadence of the Mayas. When the Spaniards arrived, they found a poor and divided territory that had lost its ancient grandeur. After the Conquest, the Maya of the Yucatán Peninsula became quite hostile and made their region one of the most impenetrable "regions of refuge." This was mainly the result of the isolation of the Mayan zone from the central part of New Spain, the tremendous exploitation they suffered from owners of henequen plantations in Yucatán and coffee plantations in the Soconusco region of Chiapas, and the emergence among the peninsular Maya of the system of independent *caciques* (bosses) in the middle of the nineteenth century. This eventually led to the "caste war" that devastated the peninsula for several decades and had repercussions in the Chiapas highlands, where several rebellions broke out. The situation has changed completely since 1930, when land reform, suppression of plantations, and programs of induced acculturation began to produce integration of Mayan groups into the national culture. Some isolated groups, however, have resisted acculturation and still live as in ancient times.

◄ The creators of the great Mayan civilization, that began three thousand years ago, still live in the face of this woman, one of the 280 remaining Lacandons of Chiapas. They may be considered "living reliefs," so much do they resemble pre-Hispanic Mayan stelae figures.

Most Lacandon dwellings, like their temples, are built without walls because of the intense heat. Various kinds of wood are used for the framework, which is roofed with palm leaves. The Lacandons make their apparel from cloth obtained from bartering with visiting European travelers, and some even wear European dress. In ancient times they made a certain kind of ceremonial dress by beating the bark of the *majagua* tree by hand and then decorating it with vegetable pigments. Now they make this dress only for important religious ceremonies.

ECONOMY. Economics help to define some of these differences among the Mayan peoples. In northern Yucatán, for example, henequen is cultivated on collective farms. Almost no food crops are grown because of the nature of the soil. Many of the inhabitants also work at industrial tasks such as the manufacture of henequen fiber and rope; therefore theirs is a market economy. In contrast, the Lacandons, who are isolated and dispersed throughout the Chiapas forests, cultivate maize by means of a *roza* (clearing) system. The groups in the Chiapas highlands maintain a permanent economic relationship with the mestizos, to whom they sell their agricultural products and from whom they acquire merchandise in a trade relationship usually disadvantageous to them. The Chontal communities of Tabasco are isolated for several months by the rainy season and are forced to rely on their own resources. During the dry season they establish commercial relations with the mestizos, from whom they obtain essential goods in exchange for fish, bananas, and palm-leaf hats, which are their principal sources of income.

HANDICRAFTS. A variety of handicrafts are produced by the Mayan groups. On the Yucatán Peninsula the indigenous groups manufacture products from henequen, weave hats, and embroider cotton. The Chontals and Lacandons make vessels from gourds and decorate them with incised work. In the Chiapas highlands, handicrafts are richer, for wool and cotton are woven and embroidered, musical instruments

◄ The Lacandons, a very solitary Maya group, travel by overland paths cut through the jungle, or by dugout canoes propelled along the rivers and lakes, which traverse their territory, with roughly carved paddles and long poles. The canoes are blessed in a special ceremony.

A museum showcase contains Lacandon idols and implements used in hunting, fishing, and making clothes. Among the surviving Indian populations of Mexico, the Lacandons are exceptionally pure and few in number. Not surprisingly, they are polygamous. Wives live together in the same house, share the domestic tasks, and help their husband in his work. Both men and women wear their hair long. They are relatively clear-skinned, of wide nose, and have thicker lips than most Indian groups. They are poor, but quite friendly. Their technological level is low, and they live under primitive, jungle conditions. The illustrations indicate the way of life of these astonishing people, who seem to have come out of a far distant past when European civilization had not yet touched the New World.

The propitiatory *balché* rite of the Lacandons has many aims: to bring rain, to prevent disaster, to cure the sick. The photo-mural in the museum shows three aspects of this communal rite. On the left, the ritual beverage is made from the juice of the sugar cane and the bark of the *balché* shrub, while a dignitary uses a fire drill to prepare the sacred fire for the ritual. In the center is the ceremony, in which the adult men sing prayers, smoke, and drink *balché* before lighted braziers in the "Houses of the Gods," which women are forbidden to enter. On the right, participants in the rite paint their faces, arms, legs, and tunics with yellowish-red *achiote*. Brazier gods, used for burning *pom* (turpentine) during the ceremonies, are exhibited before the mural. The "gods" are molded of clay, dried in the sun, baked, and decorated with red and black lines on a white background. The *luch* (ceremonial gourds) to hold *balché* have incised anthropomorphic and solar decorations. When the "gods" become old and lose their magic powers, or otherwise fall from favor, the Lacandons break them and immediately create new ones.

such as guitars, harps, and marimbas are manufactured, and pottery is made. However, in comparison with other indigenous groups, Mayan handicrafts are some of the poorest and least varied of the Republic.

DWELLING. The variety in house construction is very considerable. Houses range from rectangular mud and wattle huts, with thatched and pitched roofs, to constructions of stone, brick, and cement, built by the more acculturated peoples.

RELIGION. The Maya of the henequen zone have adopted the national religious practices. Formally they are Catholics, although they preserve the customs of their ancient tradition. The more conservative groups celebrate agricultural ceremonies such as the *Cha-Chaac* to propitiate the rain gods. They preserve some ancient customs in the worship of the dead and in a considerable body of myths, which are rapidly being lost. The penetration of Catholic and Protestant Christianity is evident in the Chiapas highlands, but in these areas religion is impregnated with ideas and practices of pre-Hispanic tradition. The Lacandons, because of their isolation, still have a polytheistic religion, with ritual manifestations of purest pre-Hispanic Mayan origin.

The *Cha-Chaac* ceremony of the Maya from Tusik, in the Territory of Quintana Roo, is carried out when the rains are late. Once a year the men make a three-day invocation to Chaac who in Mayan culture corresponds to Tlaloc of the high plateau.

A typical house of the Mayan areas of Yucatán, Campeche, and Quintana Roo was built in the Museum. The henequen plant is shown as the symbol of the region, for it has been cultivated by many Maya since ancient times. Until the development of synthetic fibers, these areas produced over a third of the world's supply of henequen.

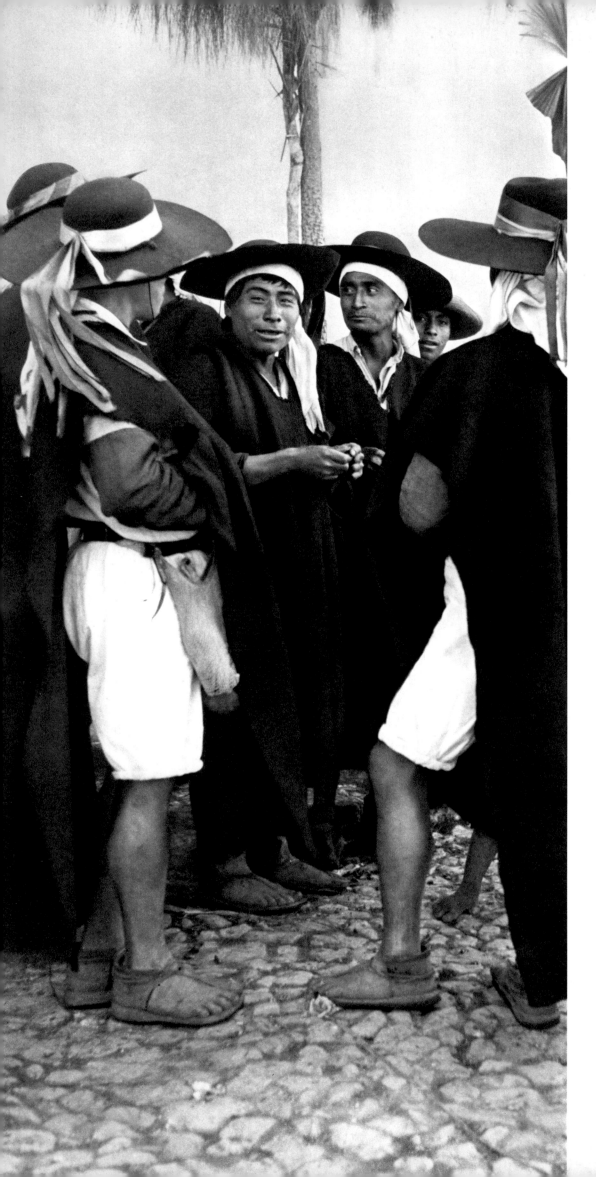

San Juan Chamula (*opposite*, *above*) is the most important ceremonial center for the Maya of Chiapas. In this town are the church, the school, the municipal seat, and the market. The Tzotzil people gather here on New Year's Day, when the transfer of governors is carried out. Tzotzil authorities of San Andres Larrainzar, Chiapas, arrive (*left*) in official dress —long black tunics, headbands, and felt hats. The outgoing authorities greet the incoming ones (*opposite*, *left*) with ritual speeches, before handing over the staff of office. The *Mayores* (elders) tie together bundles of staves, representing power, and place them in a circle before the authorities. Their wives (*opposite*, *right*), sit in front of the bundles, guarding them until they are safely in the hands of the new leaders. One of the distinct features of pre-Columbian Maya society was its sense of social hierarchy and tradition. The preservation of these features is clearly demonstrated in the ceremonies seen here, which attest to the Mayas' enduring love of social order.

ETHNOGRAPHY OF NORTHWESTERN MEXICO

REGION. Northwestern Mexico comprises the states of Baja California and Sonora, the Territory of Baja California, the northern part of the state of Sinaloa, and the western section of the state of Chihuahua. The coast and the central part of the area consist of plains, while the rugged western Sierra Madre rise in the east. The high parts of the Sierra have heavy snowfalls, at times three feet deep, and are covered with coniferous forests. The warm climate in the deep canyons produces much tropical vegetation. Intensive rainfall swells the rivers, which flow down the canyons and empty into the plains. To the north the plains form one of the most desolate and inhospitable deserts in the world, the Sonora Arizona—hot, dry, and covered with cactus and spiny brushwood that blossoms exuberantly in summer when the rivers flow down from the mountains. Dams have converted the plains into fertile valleys.

POPULATION. There are three types of indigenous cultures based on agriculture in northwestern Mexico: desert culture, which includes the Cucapas, Quilingua, Pai-Pai, Cochimi, Seri, and Papago Indians, of whom the Seri will serve as an example; mountain cultivators, including the Tarahumara, Tubare, Guariji, and Pima Indians, of whom the Tarahumara will be the example; and plains farmers, made up of the Yaqui, Maya, Opata, and Jova Indians, represented here by the Yaqui. The Seri Indians, who number only 280 people, have lived in Desemboque and Punta Chueca on the desert coast of Sonora for more or less long periods, but are basically nomadic. The Tarahumaras number more than 70,000 and inhabit the most rugged part of the western Sierra Madre in western Chihuahua. The Yaqui Indians number 10,000 and inhabit eight towns along the banks of the Yaqui River.

LANGUAGE. The Yaqui and Tarahumara Indians speak languages of the Uto-Aztec family, while the Seri language belongs to the Macro-Yuma family. Some groups in the northwestern section of Mexico have already lost their native tongues, although they sometimes retain indigenous cultural traits. Among these groups are the Tubare, Opata, and Jova Indians.

HISTORY. Before the Conquest, the groups inhabiting northwestern Mexico had to adapt themselves to their environment. Those of the desert culture lived by gathering food and by fishing and hunting in small groups throughout the region; the mountain cultivators planted with the seasonal rains, using the slopes of the mountains and small plateaus for their plots; the plains farmers of the south took advantage of the swollen rivers to plant their crops. In the seventeenth century Jesuit missionaries arrived in the region, intent on bringing Christianity to the Tarahumara Indians, but they had little success. This is perhaps because in the eighteenth and nineteenth centuries Tarahumara lands were invaded by mestizos and creoles; bloody rebellions followed, and the Tarahumara Indians took refuge in the most inhospitable Sierra, where they remain today. Before the Conquest, the Yaqui Indians were semi-nomadic hunters and farmers who fought off the Spanish several times. In the seventeenth century the Jesuits arrived among them, pacified and proselytized them, and left a mark that still exists today. Soon after the

◄ The Tarahumaras from the western Sierra Madre are known as great runners. Here a group of Tarahumara musicians huddle beneath their blankets in the cold mountain air, and play primitive homemade violins while waiting for one of their famous foot races to end.

independence of Mexcio, the Yaqui Indians again rebelled, but during the regime of Porfirio Díaz they were decimated and even deported *en masse* to other regions of the Republic. The lands taken away from them were restored in part by General Lázaro Cárdenas during his term in office (1934-1940).

ECONOMY. In the desert, bordered by the sea, the Seri Indians have developed an economy of constant nomadism. Although they now live more or less permanently in Desemboque and Punta Chueca, they still go into the desert on occasion to gather *pitahaya* and other fruits; they establish themselves close to desert water holes, where they obtain the fiber *torote*, which is used in their basketwork. They also obtain *caguama* (giant tortoise) and other marine life. The Tarahumara Indians cultivate maize in plots called *magüechic*, but soil erosion forces them to move constantly from place to place. In winter they go down the deepest places of the Sierra to escape the cold; they can also be considered nomads. At times they settle next to their plots, but they travel to ceremonial centers for Sunday assemblies and for *tesgüinadas*, which regulate cooperative work and festivals and games: thus the unity of the group is preserved. The economy of the Yaqui Indians is now highly mechanized, and their territory is one of the most important agricultural areas in the nation. The indigenous peoples, however, have little to do with agricultural labor because of political and administrative factors. The lack of agricultural tasks permits them to devote themselves to the political-administrative and religious matters of their tribes.

HANDICRAFTS. The Seri women manufacture *coritas* (heart-shaped baskets) from the *torote* plant. In ancient times these were ornamented with geometric designs, but the more modern baskets have floral decorations. The Tarahumara Indians manufacture wooden farming implements, yokes for oxen, and a rather rough pottery. The Yaqui manufacture very rudimentary rush mats and reed baskets.

DWELLING. The nomadic Seri Indians live outdoors; the entwined branch shelters they build to give themselves some shade in the desert offer little protection against the climate. These shelters are about thirteen feet square and no more than five feet high. The Tarahumara Indians live in caves with stone divisions inside, although sometimes they build stone houses. The farther south one goes in Chihuahua, toward the region of the Tepehua Indians, the more frequently one sees log and stone houses. The Yaqui Indians have houses with three quadrangular sections; the interior structure is of mezquite planted in the soil, and vertical and horizontal branches of that tree are laced onto it. The walls are made of reeds woven vertically and horizontally and tied with cords.

RELIGION. The Seri Indians preserve something of their pre-Hispanic religion. They worship such gods as the god of the center of the earth, represented as a mole, the god of the seas, and the god of the hills. Their main festivals are held in May when the giant tortoise arrives on the coastline and in July when the gathering of *pitahaya* begins. Both events are celebrated by the reunion of the tribe to eat giant tortoise or *pitahaya* honey, and they dance and sing until dawn. The Tarahumaras retain beliefs of pre-Hispanic origin mixed with Christian influences. They hold festivals with certain religious connotations by which they regulate their ritual calendar. These include the peyote ceremony, related to the agricultural deities, who are the predominant numens in their pantheon. Moreover, the exhausting foot races called *dahipu* are famous and important in their social activity; men run barefoot and kick a wooden ball along tracks several miles long. The Yaqui religion is also a strange mixture of indigenous and Christian ideas. Like the Tarahumaras, Yaquis have their council of elders. An *alahuatzin*, or whipper, gives public lashings to those receiving punishment, and a military force includes captains, commanders, lieutenants, sergeants, corporals, and regular troops. The *comunila*, whose decisions are carried out by the "governors," organizes religious festivals, which are then entrusted to the *Yo'owes*, roughly equivalent to the Catholic priests.

◄ In winter the Sierra Madre mountains are covered with as much as three feet of snow, and the Tarahumara Indians retreat to the temperate warmth of the deep ravines. When winter ends, they return to plant the steeply inclined plots of land for the yearly maize crop.

Two Tarahumara youths wait at the roadside for the runners to pass. One of them is carving a wooden ball to be used in the races. Both wear traditional costumes. Their sandals consist of leather soles (now often a piece of automobile tire) tied with thongs.

The Tarahumaras, a mountain-cultivating people from the western Sierra Madre, have been known as great runners since ancient times. The Aztecs often employed them as messengers. They still hold regular foot races, and greatly admire physical skill and grace. Two teams race, each kicking a ball before them. Traditional rules govern the event, and the team wins which has the greater number of runners left at the time limit agreed upon—from a few hours to three days and nights. Women also race (*opposite*), but their contests are not as long or as important, and instead of kicking a ball they roll a hoop with sticks.

A Tarahumara woman's loose blouse reflects the Spanish influence; until the eighteenth century these women wore only loose skirts held at the waist by a sash and headbands like those of the men. During the winter, they wear as many as five blouses and skirts, and a shawl in which babies are carried.

The Seri are a tough, nomadic Indian group, who live mostly on the coast of Sonora and on the Tiburón island. Their habitat is a desert near the sea. They are essentially of a hunting and fishing culture that, until recently, still refused the use of the knife and fire. They have firmly resisted all attempts to integrate them into national society. The Seri, like the Tarahumaras, are known for their physical strength and power. They are tall, athletic, graceful, and are trained to be fighters. A Seri harpooner here rests in the prow of his boat, as it returns to the coast, probably after an expedition to catch giant tortoise. His dress is mestizo, but he retains characteristically long hair. Formerly, these Indians wore an apron of donkey, deer or pelican skin.

In the museum Seri fishing equipment and photographs of their way of ▶ life provide the background for three pieces of Tarahumara pottery. The large pot decorated with strips of reeds is used for fermenting corn to make the beverage *tesguiño*. The smaller ones, of gray clay decorated with red geometric designs, closely resemble the pottery of the Mogollon and Hohokam Indian groups in the southwestern United States.

The ritual marking the beginning of puberty for a young Seri girl is held in Desemboque, Sonora. An older woman paints the girl's face, leads her into the water fully dressed, and washes her head. During the ceremony, which begins in the afternoon, there are games and feasting, and dancing.

In the museum, models of Yaqui dancers, called *pascolas* ("little old men of the fiesta") represent this forest fertility dance with movements that recall the alertness of the deer. The *pascolas* are accompanied by guitar, harp, and singers who, like the dancers, wear masks that cover either their faces or the sides of their heads. In the background are the musical instruments used to accompany the *pascolas'* dance of the deer: the European harp and violin and the traditional Indian cane flutes, water drums, scrapers, rattles, and *tenábaris*. Both these dances are performed at the festival of the patron saint of the village, on Christmas and New Year's Day, during Holy Week, and at ceremonies commemorating the death of an important Yaqui chief.

The deer, which represents the spirit of the forest, is incarnated in the traditional Yaqui deer dancer, who imitates the graceful movements ▶ of the animal in its free state, to the accompaniment of a scraper and flute. He carries rattles in his hands, and tied around his legs are *tenábaris*, dried butterfly cocoons, which also rattle as he dances. His delicate mask and turban are topped by the head of a young deer.

THE SYNTHESIS OF MEXICO

In the Archaeological rooms, on the main floor of the museum, and in the Ethnographic rooms on the floor above, the visitor will have seen those achievements of the pre-Hispanic cultures of Mexico and such vestiges of the old Indian cultures that still survive in certain remote regions of the country. Now, in this room, the Synthesis of Mexico, the visitor may observe what elements of the ancient civilizations have become a part of the life and culture of the present day Mexican. The fact is that the old cultures were simply neither wiped out by the wave of violence of the Conquest, nor brought to attrition by centuries of colonialism. Rather, fusing with European elements, the old Indian cultures created the basis and shaped the characteristic aspects of contemporary Mexican life.

Examples of this Indian influence are shown in architecture and city planning. The great squares of Mexico, Cholula and Tepeaca indicate the plans of cities which to begin with were Indian. The original length and directions of its streets, for instance, continue to give Mexico City much of its present character. Building materials, such as *tezontle* and *chiluca*, basalt and tecali, dating back to the most ancient times, continue to be used in the nation's modern buildings. Native architectural styles of subsequent development, such as the plateresque, as shown in the decoration of the convents of Acolmán and Tecamachalco, reflect the spirit of the Indian craftsmen. It should come as no surprise that contemporary painters like Rivera, Orozco, Siqueiros or Tamayo should reveal in one way or another the Indian impact upon the form, color, composition and, particularly, the spirit of their work. And what is so easily seen in the architecture and painting of the country is also observable in the dance, the music, and even the literature of thought and imagination. The same thing is even more obviously true of the folk arts.

But the growing consciousness of this past and present in the life and culture of the nation is the manifestation of another fact of tremendous political and social consequences. It is now common knowledge that since the political and social transformation brought about by the Mexican Revolution of 1910, the Indian has ceased to be a man attached to his old pre-historic traditions; it has become known that he too is a dynamic element in a new history, since he now utilizes modern techniques to attain a better economy, more effective care of his health and that of his children, a greater communication with others of his kind by means of modern roads, and in short an education each day more complete of himself. Various programs of education and integration have brought him quickly into the twentieth century. Especially important has been a far-reaching program of education by means of pre-fabricated schools, shipped to the most remote parts of the land. As literacy increases, the balance between conservation of age-old customs and the ways of the modern world become increasingly more delicate.

In brief, every true revolution is a struggle for a new kind of consciousness and although a new political party, new labour or agrarian reform laws and other social improvements may be the expressions of this new consciousness, the fact remains that the basic character of the Mexican Revolution, its essential value, is that it made the Mexican conscious of himself. It is for this reason that the Synthesis of Mexico is the last room in the museum. In it is shown not only the assimilation so far achieved of the Indian in the national life, but also his projection upon the future of the country. It has the logic of the inevitable that Benito Juárez should preside over this room. He was an Indian capable of securing the independence of Mexico, for, rising from humble shepherd origins, he rose to become president of the country, thus achieving once and for all the recognition of the historical destiny of the nation: the integration of the three elements of its culture, the Indian, the colonial, and the modern. Thus, even before they had attained the consciousness of their role, the Indian populations began to act in the process of becoming fundamental elements in the progress of the country.

◄ The Synthesis of Mexico Room offers the visitor a panoramic view of the pre-Columbian and European elements that combine to give contemporary Mexico its characteristic identity as a nation and a culture.

NOTES

SELECTED BIBLIOGRAPHY

ARCHAEOLOGY OF MEXICO

AVELEYRA ARROYO DE ANDA, LUIS.
"Pre-Columbian Art in the new National Museum of Anthropology in Mexico City," *The Connoisseur*, CLX, No. 644 (October, 1965), pp. 91-101.

— and GROTH-KIMBALL, IRMGARD.
Obras selectas del arte prehispánico: adquisiciones recientes. (Consejo para la planeación e instalación del Museo Nacional de Antropología.) Mexico. Secretaría de Educación Pública, 1964.

BERNAL, IGNACIO.
Bibliografía de arqueología y etnografía: Mesoamérica y Norte de México, 1514-1960. (Instituto Nacional de Antropología e Historia, Memorias VII.) Mexico. Instituto Nacional de Antropología e Historia, 1962.

— *Mexican Wall-paintings of the Maya and Aztec Periods.* New York. The New American Library of World Literature, Inc., 1963.

BURLAND, COTTIE A.
Art and Life in Ancient Mexico. Oxford. B. Cassirer, 1948.

CASO, ALFONSO.
The Aztecs; People of the Sun. Translated by L. Dunham. Norman, Okla. University of Oklahoma Press, 1958.

— and BERNAL, IGNACIO.
Urnas de Oaxaca (Instituto Nacional de Antropología e Historia, Memorias II.) 2 vols. Mexico. Instituto Nacional de Antropología e Historia, 1952.

COE, MICHAEL D.
Mexico. New York. Frederick A. Praeger, Inc., 1962.

COVARRUBIAS, MIGUEL.
Mezcala: Ancient Mexican Sculpture. New York. André Emmerich Gallery, 1956.

— *Indian Art of Mexico and Central America.* New York. Alfred A. Knopf, Inc., 1957.

DISSELHOFF, HANS D., and LINNÉ, SIGVALD.
The Art of Ancient America. New York. Crown Publishers, Inc., 1960.

DOCKSTADER, FREDERICK J., and GUADAGNO, CARMELO.
Indian Art in Middle America. Greenwich, Conn. New York Graphic Society, 1964.

EMMERICH, ANDRÉ, and BOLTIN, LEE.
Art Before Columbus. New York. Simon and Schuster, Inc., 1963.

FLORES GUERRERO, RAÚL.
Historia general del arte mexicano: Epoca prehispánica. Mexico. Editorial Hermes, 1962.

— *Flor y canto del arte prehispánico de México.* Mexico. Banco Nacional de Comercio Exterior, 1964.

GROTH-KIMBALL, IRMGARD.
Mayan Terra-cottas. New York. Frederick A. Praeger, Inc., 1960.

— and FEUCHTWANGER, FRANZ.
The Art of Ancient Mexico. London and New York. Thames and Hudson, 1954.

KELEMAN, PÁL.
Medieval American Art. New ed. New York. The Macmillan Company, 1956.

KRICKEBERG, WALTER.
Altmexikanische Kulturen. Berlin. Safari-Verlag, 1956.

KUBLER, GEORGE.
The Art and Architecture of Ancient America. Baltimore. Penguin Books, Inc., 1962.

LEHMANN, HENRI.
L'art précolombien. Paris. Masson et Cie, 1960

LEÓN-PORTILLA, MIGUEL.
Los antiguos Mexicanos, a través de sus crónicas y cantares. Mexico. Fondo de Cultura Económica, 1961.

LOTHROP, SAMUEL K.
Treasures of Ancient America. Geneva. Albert Skira, 1964.

— et al. *Pre-Columbian Art: Robert Woods Bliss Collection.* London. Phaidon Press, Ltd., 1957.

MARQUINA, IGNACIO.
Arquitectura prehispánica. (Instituto Nacional de Antropología e Historia, Memorias I.) 2nd ed. Mexico. Secretaría de Educación Pública, 1964.

MORLEY, SYLVANUS G.
The Ancient Maya. Stanford, Calif. Stanford University Press, 1946.

NOGUERA, EDUARDO.
La cerámica arqueológica de Mesoamérica. (Instituto de Investigaciones Históricas, 1a. Serie, No. 86.) Mexico. Universidad Nacional Autónoma de México, 1965.

NORIEGA, RAÚL, et al.
Esplendor del México antiguo. 2 vols. Mexico. Centro de Investigaciones Antropológicas de México, 1959.

PETERSON, FREDERICK A.
Ancient Mexico: An Introduction to the Pre-Hispanic Cultures. New York. G. P. Putnam's Sons, 1959.

PIÑA CHAN, ROMÁN.
Las culturas preclásicas de la Cuenca de México. Mexico. Fondo de Cultura Económica, 1955.

— *Mesoamérica; ensayo, histórico cultural.* (Instituto Nacional de Antropología e Historia, Memorias VI.) Mexico. Instituto Nacional de Antropología e Historia, 1960.

— and COVARRUBIAS, LUIS.
El pueblo del jaguar: Los Olmecas arqueológicos. (Consejo para la planeación e instalación del Museo Nacional de Antropología.) Mexico. Secretaría de Educación Pública, 1964

PROSKOURIAKOFF, TATIANA A.
An Album of Maya Architecture. New ed. Norman, Okla. University of Oklahoma Press, 1963.

— *A Study of Classic Maya Sculpture.* (Carnegie Institution of Washington, Pub. 593.) Washington, D.C. Carnegie Institution of Washington, 1950.

RIVET, PAUL.
Maya Cities. Translated by M. and L. Kochan. New York. G. P. Putnam's Sons, 1960.

— and FREUND, GISÈLE.
Mexique précolombien. (Collection des Ides Photographiques, 8.) Neuchâtel. Éditions Ides et calendes, 1954.

RUBÍN DE LA BORBOLLA, DANIEL.
"Guerrero: The Mystery of the Green-stone Sculptors," *Art News Annual,* XXX (1965), pp. 82-95.

RUZ LHUILLIER, ALBERTO.
La civilización de los antiguos Mayas. (Instituto Nacional de Antropología e Historia, Serie Historia X.) Mexico. Instituto Nacional de Antropología e Historia, 1963.

SAVILLE, MARSHALL H.
The Goldsmith's Art in Ancient Mexico. (Indian Notes and Monographs, Miscellaneous No. 7.) New York. Museum of the American Indian; Heye Foundation, 1920.

— *Turquoise Mosaic Art in Ancient Mexico.* (Museum of the American Indian; Heye Foundation; Contributions from the Heye Museum, VI.) New York. Museum of the American Indian, 1922.

— *The Wood-carver's Art in Ancient Mexico.* (Museum of the American Indian; Heye Foundation; Contributions from the Heye Museum, IX.) New York. Museum of the American Indian, 1925.

SOUSTELLE, JACQUES.
The Daily Life of the Aztecs, on the Eve of the Spanish Conquest. Translated by P. O'Brian. New York. The Macmillan Company, 1962.

SPINDEN, HERBERT J.
A Study of Maya Art, its Subject Matter and Historical Development. (Peabody Museum of American Archaeology and Ethnology, Memoirs VI.) Cambridge, Mass. The Museum, 1913.

SPRATLING, WILLIAM.
Más humano que divino. Mexico. Universidad Nacional Autónoma de México, 1960.

STIERLIN, HENRI, and RAMÍREZ VÁZQUEZ, PEDRO.
Maya: Guatemala, Honduras et Yucatán. Fribourg. Architecture Universelle, Office du Livre, 1964.

THOMPSON, ERIC S.
The Rise and Fall of Maya Civilization. Norman, Okla. University of Oklahoma Press, 1954.

TOSCANO, SALVADOR.
Arte precolombino de México y de la América Central. (Instituto de Investigaciones Estéticas.) 2nd ed. Mexico. Universidad Nacional Autónoma de México, 1951.

VAILLANT, GEORGE C.
Aztecs of Mexico: Origin, Rise and Fall of the Aztec Nation. Garden City, N.Y. Doubleday & Company, Inc., 1962.

VILLARET, BERNARD.
"Figures de Jaina, suprême expression de l'art Maya," *Connaissance des Arts,* No. 90 (August, 1959), pp. 46-51.

WESTHEIM, PAUL.
Arte antiguo de México. Mexico. Fondo de Cultura Económica, 1950.

— *Ideas fundamentales del arte prehispánico en México.* Mexico. Fondo de Cultura Económica, 1957.

— *La cerámica del Mexico antiguo.* (Colección de Arte, No. 11.) Mexico. Universidad Nacional Autónoma de México, 1962.

— *The Sculpture of Ancient Mexico.* Translated by M. Frenk. Garden City, N.Y. Doubleday & Company, Inc., 1963.

ETHNOLOGY OF MEXICO

AGUIRRE BELTRÁN, GONZALO.
Formas de gobierna indígena. Mexico. Imprenta Universitaria, 1953.

AUGUR, HELEN.
Zapotec. Garden City, N.Y. Doubleday & Company, Inc., 1954.

BASAURI, CARLOS.
La población indígena de México. 3 vols. Mexico. Secretaría de Educación Pública, 1940.

BEALS, RALPH L.
The Comparative Ethnology of Northern Mexico before 1750. Berkeley, Calif. University of California Press, 1932.

— *Ethnology of the Western Mixe.* Berkeley, Calif. University of California Press, 1945.

— *Cherán: A Sierra Tarascan Village.* (Institute of Social Anthropology, Pub. No. 2.) Washington, D.C. Smithsonian Institution, 1946.

BENNETT, WENDELL C., and ZINGG, ROBERT M.
  The Tarahumara, an Indian Tribe of Northern Mexico.
  Chicago. University of Chicago Press, 1935.

BUNZEL, RUTH L.
  " The Role of Alcoholism in Two Central American
  Communities, " *Psychiatry,* II, No. 3 (1940), pp. 361-87.

CARRASCO, PEDRO.
  Tarascan Folk Religion. (Middle American Research
  Institute, Pub. 17.) New Orleans. Tulane University,
  1952.

CASO, ALFONSO.
  " New World Culture History : Middle America, "
  Anthropology Today (International Symposium on An-
  thropology, N.Y., 1952). Chicago. University of
  Chicago Press, 1953, pp. 226-37.

CERDA SILVA, ROBERTO DE LA, ROJAS GONZALÉZ, FRAN-
  CISCO, and BARRAGÁN AVILÉS, RENÉ.
  Etnografía de México. Síntesis monográfica. (Instituto de
  Investigaciones Sociales.) Mexico. Universidad Na-
  cional Autónoma de México, 1957.

CHEVALIER, FRANÇOIS.
  Land and Society in Colonial Mexico : The Great Hacienda.
  Berkeley, Calif. University of California Press, 1963.

COOK, SHERBURNE F.
  Santa Maria Ixcatlán. Berkeley, Calif. University of
  California Press, 1958.

— and SIMPSON, LESLEY B.
  The Population of Central Mexico in the Sixteenth Century.
  Berkeley, Calif. University of California Press, 1948.

CORTES, HERNAN.
  Five Letters. Translated by J. Bayard Morris. New York.
  W.W. Norton & Company, Inc., 1962.

FOSTER, GEORGE M.
  Empire's Children : Tzintzuntzán. (Institute of Social
  Anthropology, Pub. 6.) Mexico. Imprenta Nuevo
  Mundo, 1948.

— " Cofradía and Compadrazgo in Spain and Spanish
  America, " *Southwestern Journal of Anthropology,* IX,
  No. 1 (1953), pp. 1-26.

— " Cultural Responses to Expressions of Envy in Tzintzuntzán, " *Southwestern Journal of Anthropology,* XXI,
  No. 1 (1965), pp. 24-35.

FUENTE, JULIO DE LA.
  Yalalag, una villa zapoteca serrana. (Museo Nacional de
  Antropología. Serie cientifica 1.) Mexico. Instituto
  Nacional de Antropología e Historia, 1949.

GIBSON, CHARLES.
  The Aztecs under Spanish Rule. Stanford, Calif. Stanford
  University Press, 1964.

GILLEN, JOHN.
  " Magical Fright, " *Psychiatry,* XI, No. 4 (1948), pp. 387-
  400.

GUITERAS-HOLMES, CALIXTA.
  Perils of the Soul ; The World View of a Tzotzil Indian.
  New York. The Free Press of Glencoe, 1961.

HANKE, LEWIS.
  Bartolomé de las Casas. Philadelphia. University of
  Pennsylvania Press, 1952.

KELLY, ISABEL T., and PALERM, ANGEL.
  *The Tajín Totonac and other Zapotec-speaking Pueblos of
  Oaxaca, Mexico.* Washington, D.C. Smithsonian Insti-
  tution, 1952.

LEÓN-PORTILLA, MIGUEL (ed.).
  *The Broken Spears ; The Aztec Account of the Conquest of
  Mexico.* Translated by L. Kemp. Boston. Beacon
  Press, 1962.

LESLIE, CHARLES.
  *Now We are Civilized : A Study of the World View of the
  Zapotec Indians of Mitla, Oaxaca.* Detroit, Mich. Wayne
  University Press, 1960.

LEWIS, OSCAR.
  Life in a Mexican Village : Tepoztlán Restudied. Urbana,
  III. University of Illinois Press, 1951.

— " Mexico since Cárdenas, " *Social Change of Latin America Today.* Edited by R. Adams, *et al.* New York.
  Vintage Books, Inc., Alfred A. Knopf, Inc., 1960,
  pp. 285-345.

LOTHROP, SAMUEL K., *et al.* (eds.).
  The Maya and Their Neighbors. New York. D. Appleton-
  Century Company, Inc., 1940. (Reprint, Salt Lake
  City. University of Utah Press, 1962.)

LUMHOLTZ, KARL.
  Unknown Mexico. 2 vols. New York. Charles Scribner's
  Sons, 1902.

MADSEN, WILLIAM.
  The Virgin's Children in an Aztec Village Today. Austin,
  Tex. University of Texas Press, 1960.

NADER, LAURA, and METZGER, DUANE.
  " Conflict Resolution in Two Mexican Communities, "
  American Anthropologist, LXV (1963), pp. 584-92.

PALERM, ANGEL, and WOLF, ERIC.
  " La agricultura y el desarrollo de la civilización en
  Mesoamérica, " *Revista Interaméricana de Ciencias Sociales,*
  I, No. 2 (1961).

PARSON, ELSIE C.
  Mitla, Town of the Souls. Chicago. University of
  Chicago Press, 1936.

POZAS, RICARDO.
  Juan, the Chamula. Berkeley, Calif. University of California Press, 1962.

RAVICZ, ROBERT S.
  Organización social de los Mixtecos. (Colección de Antro-
  pología Social, No. 5.) Mexico. Instituto Nacional
  Indigenista, 1965.

REDFIELD, ROBERT.
  Tepoztlán ; A Mexican Village. Chicago. University of
  Chicago Press, 1930.

— *The Folk Cultures of Yucatán.* Chicago. University of
  Chicago Press, 1941.

— and VILLA ROJAS, ALFONSO.
Chan Kom, A Maya Village. (Carnegie Institution of Washington, Pub. 448.) Washington, D.C. Carnegie Institution of Washington, 1934.

RICARD, ROBERT.
La " Conquête spirituelle " du Mexique. (Université de Paris, Institut d'Ethnologie, Travaux et Mémoires, XX.) Paris. Institut d'Ethnologie, 1933.

ROMNEY, ANTON K.
" The Mixtecans of Juxtlahuaca, Mexico, " *Six Cultures, Studies of Child Rearing.* Edited by B. Whiting. New York. John Wiley & Sons, Inc., 1963.

SAHAGÚN, BERNARDINO DE.
General History of the Things of New Spain. Florentine Codex. Translated and edited by A. J. O. Anderson and C. Dibble. (Monographs of the School of American Research, No. 14.) 10 vols. Salt Lake City. University of Utah Press, 1950-61.

SIMPSON, LESLEY BYRD.
Many Mexicos. 2nd ed. New York. G. P. Putnam's Sons, 1946.

— *The Encomienda in New Spain; The Beginning of Spanish Mexico.* Rev. ed. Berkeley, Calif. University of California Press, 1950.

SOUSTELLE, JACQUES.
La famille otomi-pame du Mexique Central. (Université de Paris, Institut d'Ethnologie, Travaux et Mémoires, XXVI.) Paris. Institut d'Ethnologie, 1937.

SPICER, EDWARD H.
Potam, a Yaqui Village in Sonora. (American Anthropological Association, Memoir No. 77.) Menasha, Wisc. American Anthropological Association, 1954.

TAX, SOL (ed.).
Heritage of Conquest; The Ethnology of Middle America. New York. The Free Press of Glencoe, 1952.

TOOR, FRANCES.
A Treasury of Mexican Folkways. New York. Crown Publishers, Inc., 1947.

TOZZER, ALFRED M.
Landa's Relacion de las cosas de Yucatán. (Peabody Museum of Archaeology and Ethnology, Papers, vol. XVIII.) Cambridge, Mass. Harvard University Press, 1941.

VILLA ROJAS, ALFONSO.
The Maya of East Central Quintana Roo. (Carnegie Institution of Washington, Pub. 559.) Washington, D.C. Carnegie Institution of Washington, 1945.

VOGT, EVON Z.
Los Zinacantecos, un pueblo tzotzil de los altos de Chiapas. Mexico. Instituto Nacional Indigenista, 1966.

WEITLANER, ROBERTO J., and CASTRO, CARLOS A.
Mayultianguiz y Tlacoatzintepec. Mexico. Instituto Nacional de Antropología e Historia, 1954.

WHETTEN, NATHAN L.
Rural Mexico. Chicago. University of Chicago Press, 1948.

WOLF, ERIC.
" Closed Corporate Peasant Communities in Mesoamerica and Central Java, " *Southwestern Journal of Anthropology*, XIII, No. 1 (1957), pp. 1-18.

— *Sons of the Shaking Earth.* Chicago. University of Chicago Press, 1959.

ZINGG, ROBERT M.
The Huichols: Primitive Artists. New York. G. E. Stechert & Company, 1937.

PHOTOGRAPHIC CREDITS

AVELEYRA, LUIS: 35 above left, below.
BOLTIN, LEE: 117, 130-1.
BREHME, ARNO: 51, 52, 57, 58 below, 113, 127, 149, 161.
CABIRERA, JORGE: 218, 219.
CHRISTENSEN, BODIL: 176, 181 below left, 188, 189, 192, 202, 206, 208, 210, 211 below, 216, 217, 227 left.
CORDRY, DONALD: 246 above.
DIAZ, ANTONIO: 18-19, 22, 23, 36 center, below left, 45.
FERNANDEZ, CARLOS: 213 above.
HALIK, ANTONIO: 47 above, 236.
KIMBALL, IRMGARD: 66 above left, above right, below left, 67, 81, 84, 92, 100, 101, 107 below, 115, 119 above, 120-1, 132 above, 133, 136, 140-1, 144, 150, 151, 156 above left, 158, 174, 175.
LECHUGA, RUTH: 186, 190, 196, 230, 233, 234 below left, below right, 235 below, 238, 239.
LEONELLI, FELIX: 35 above right, 58 above, 152, 198, 204, 205, 211 above, 212, 220 above, 236, 237 above, 247.
MARIN, JAIME: 21, 39, 46 above left, above right.
MENENDEZ, OSCAR: Courtesy of the National Museum of Anthropology, Mexico: 240.

MUNOZ, ALFONSO: 181 below right, 199, 200; Courtesy of the National Museum of Anthropology, Mexico: 40, 224, 246 below, 248.
RITTER, HANS: 54, 55, 71, 94, 153, 162, 163.
SAENZ, CARLOS: 181 above right, center right.
SALAS PORTUGAL: 31, 32.
SALGADO, MIGUEL: 74-5, 98, 105, 106, 108-9, 185, 226 above, 234-5 above, 249, 250-1.
SANCHEZ, CARLOS: Courtesy of the National Museum of Anthropology, Mexico: 220 below, 222.
SCHALKWIJK, BOB: 221, 227 right, 244, 245.
SCHEIN, JACOBO: 228, 229.
SIMELLI, FELIX: 183, 191, 197.
STUPAKOFF, OTTO: 11, 46 below left, 47 below, 48, 63, 64, 72, 73, 76, 79, 80, 82, 83, 87, 88, 89, 90, 91, 97, 99, 102, 103, 104, 107 above, 110, 114, 116, 118, 119 below, 122-3, 124, 128, 129, 132 below, 135, 137, 138, 139, 143, 155, 156 above right, 157, 164, 165, 166, 169, 170, 171, 172, 173.
URIBE, FRANCISCO: 59.
Courtesy of the NATIONAL MUSEUM OF ANTHROPOLOGY, Mexico: 203, 214, 226 below.

GEOGRAPHICAL INDEX

Abbreviations: ill. = illustrated, art = art work deriving from listed area

INDEX OF NAMES

PERSONS

GODS

INDIANS

This book was designed by Beatrice Trueblood
in association with the staff
of Helvetica Press Inc., New York City.

The production was directed
by Edita S.A. Lausanne.

Printing by

Héliogravure Centrale Lausanne and
Imprimerie Centrale Lausanne S.A.

Dust jacket by
Offset Jean Genoud S.A. Lausanne.

Bound by Van Rijmenam N.V., The Hague.

PRINTED IN SWITZERLAND

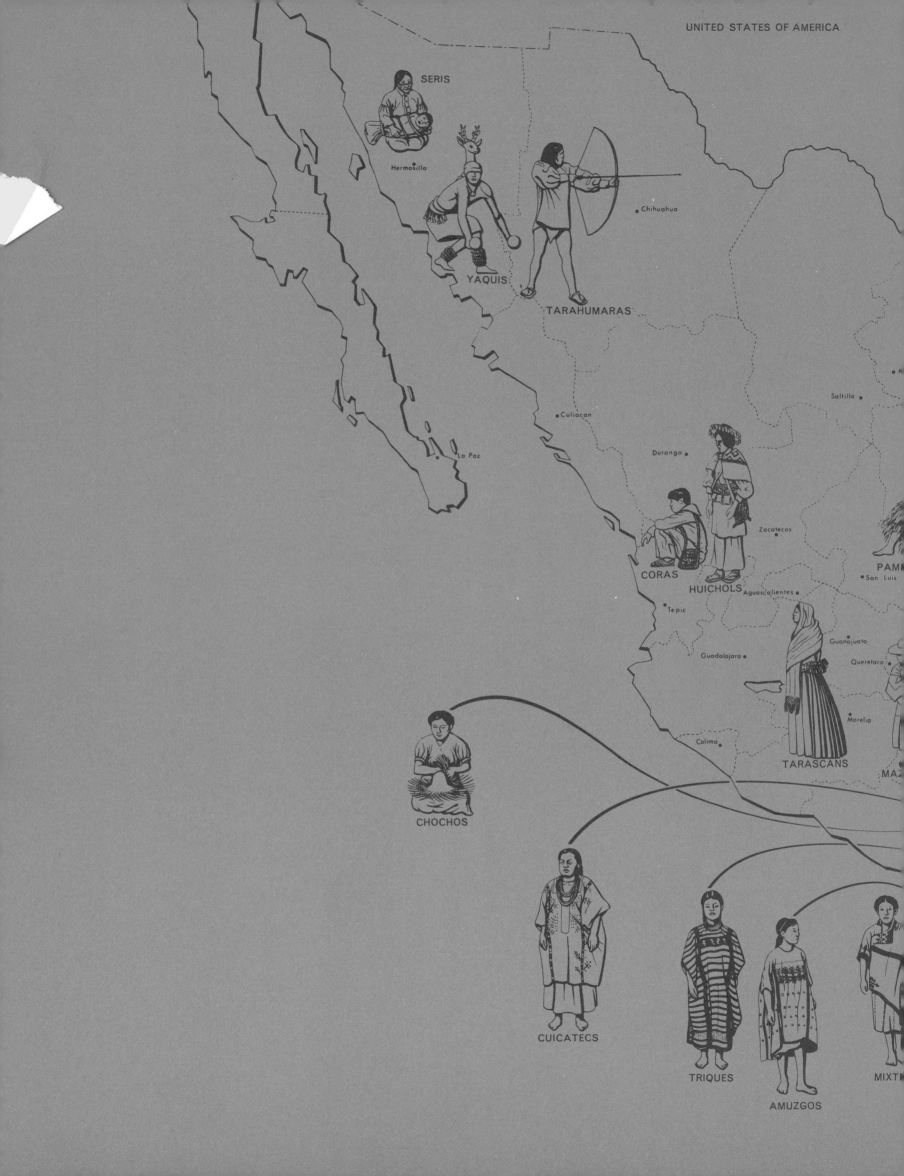

UNITED STATES OF AMERICA

SERIS

Hermosillo

YAQUIS

TARAHUMARAS

Chihuahua

Saltillo

Culiacan

Durango

Zacatecas

La Paz

CORAS

HUICHOLS

Aguascalientes

PAM

San Luis

Tepic

Guanajuato

Guadalajara

Queretaro

Colima

Morelia

TARASCANS

MA

CHOCHOS

CUICATECS

TRIQUES

MIXT

AMUZGOS